The BFRB Survival Guide

"Drs. Mouton-Odum, Golomb, and Mansueto, leaders in the field of BFRBs, have successfully crafted a user-friendly, self-guided approach to help people address their BFRBs. Based on tried and established methods, this book has potential to be a game changer for those who have struggled with and want to address their BFRB(s)."

Eric Storch, PhD, McIngvale Presidential Endowed Chair & Professor, Department of Psychiatry and Behavioral Sciences, Baylor College of Medicine

"The BFRB Survival Guide is an important follow-up to these authors' excellent guide for clinicians. It is an invaluable work and in my estimation the best and most comprehensive self-help work today for what can be a most baffling and frustrating group of disorders. Other works of this type don't even come close to its level of information and usefulness. The authors are among the top practitioners to be found in this field and, given the scarcity of specialists, a self-help work of this type is doubly important."

Fred Penzel, PhD, Psychologist and Executive Director of Western Suffolk Psychological Services, Huntington, NY

"This workbook is well organized and easy to understand, but what truly makes it stand out is how it guides the reader through the material in a personal and compassionate way – you can really feel the authors' empathy in their writing. What's especially unique is the way each exercise doesn't just end when it is completed; the authors encourage you to reflect back on the exercise, helping the insights sink in and better allowing you to integrate each experience into the bigger picture of your treatment journey. If you're struggling with BFRBs, this is a must-have resource."

Allen H. Weg, EdD, Founder, Stress and Anxiety Services; Author, *OCD Treatment Through Storytelling*

The BFRB Survival Guide

A Workbook for Overcoming Body Focused Repetitive Behaviors

Suzanne Mouton-Odum
Psychology Houston, PC-The Center for Cognitive Behavioral Treatment

Ruth Goldfinger Golomb
Behavior Therapy Center of Greater Washington

Charles S. Mansueto
Behavior Therapy Center of Greater Washington

Shaftesbury Road, Cambridge CB2 8EA, United Kingdom

One Liberty Plaza, 20th Floor, New York, NY 10006, USA

477 Williamstown Road, Port Melbourne, VIC 3207, Australia

314–321, 3rd Floor, Plot 3, Splendor Forum, Jasola District Centre, New Delhi – 110025, India

103 Penang Road, #05–06/07, Visioncrest Commercial, Singapore 238467

Cambridge University Press is part of Cambridge University Press & Assessment, a department of the University of Cambridge.

We share the University's mission to contribute to society through the pursuit of education, learning and research at the highest international levels of excellence.

www.cambridge.org
Information on this title: www.cambridge.org/9781009468503
DOI: 10.1017/9781009468466

© Suzanne Mouton-Odum, Ruth Goldfinger Golomb, and Charles S. Mansueto 2025

This publication is in copyright. Subject to statutory exception and to the provisions of relevant collective licensing agreements, no reproduction of any part may take place without the written permission of Cambridge University Press & Assessment.

When citing this work, please include a reference to the DOI 10.1017/9781009468466

First published 2025

A catalogue record for this publication is available from the British Library

A Cataloging-in-Publication data record for this book is available from the Library of Congress

ISBN 978-1-009-46850-3 Paperback

Cambridge University Press & Assessment has no responsibility for the persistence or accuracy of URLs for external or third-party internet websites referred to in this publication and does not guarantee that any content on such websites is, or will remain, accurate or appropriate.

Every effort has been made in preparing this book to provide accurate and up-to-date information that is in accord with accepted standards and practice at the time of publication. Although case histories are drawn from actual cases, every effort has been made to disguise the identities of the individuals involved. Nevertheless, the authors, editors, and publishers can make no warranties that the information contained herein is totally free from error, not least because clinical standards are constantly changing through research and regulation. The authors, editors, and publishers therefore disclaim all liability for direct or consequential damages resulting from the use of material contained in this book. Readers are strongly advised to pay careful attention to information provided by the manufacturer of any drugs or equipment that they plan to use.

For all of the brave people who have shared their stories, their wisdom, and their lived experiences with us, we dedicate this book to you.

Contents

Part I Preparation, Gaining Perspective, and Heightening Awareness of Your BFRB   1

1. Getting Started on Your BFRB Journey   3
2. Increasing Awareness of Your BFRB   36
3. Gaining a Better Understanding of Your BFRB   60

Part II Interventions and Skill Building: Selecting and Using Interventions   83

4. The Sensory Domain   85
5. The Cognitive Domain   111
6. The Affective Domain   127
7. The Motor Domain   147
8. The Place Domain   158

Part III Lifestyle Changes and Maintenance of Recovery   173

9. The Importance of Self-Care   175
10. Putting It All Together to Move Forward   198

References   208
Index   210

Part I

Preparation, Gaining Perspective, and Heightening Awareness of Your BFRB

1

Getting Started on Your BFRB Journey

Introduction to This Workbook

Congratulations on beginning your journey toward overcoming your body focused repetitive behavior. Choosing to explore this book is a step toward gaining freedom not only from the behavior itself, but from the problems that BFRBs often cause. This workbook can be used as a stand-alone manual or can also be used while you work with a therapist. We designed it as a companion to the *Comprehensive Behavioral (ComB) Treatment of Body Focused Repetitive Behaviors: A Clinical Guide* (Mansueto, Mouton-Odum, & Golomb, 2023) that we have also published to provide guidance for therapists in treating BFRBs. Regardless of whether you are working on this book alone or in conjunction with a therapist, this workbook will guide you as you strive to overcome your BFRB. It will help you understand the nature of BFRBs and hopefully put your BFRB into perspective as simply one aspect of you, but not one that defines you. How will you do this? Through gaining important awareness into your behavior (becoming very aware of all aspects of your BFRB), you will increase your knowledge about how your BFRB fits into the bigger picture of your life's activities and functions. Awareness also includes key pieces of information about the situational factors that make your BFRB more likely to occur. During this process you will come to understand how your BFRB operates in your life by identifying information about when, where, and why you engage in your BFRB. In other words, you will better understand how your behavior serves a function in your life. With this knowledge, you will be able to select and implement relevant strategies and interventions to help you in these specific situations that are difficult for you. Ultimately, we want you to find other, healthier ways to serve these important functions. Finally, as you gain momentum and begin to gain control over your BFRB, the action items here will help you to stay consistent and maintain those improvements over time, without falling back into old, unhelpful habits.

How to Use This Workbook

Think about recovery as a destination that you would like to reach or, as we present it in this workbook, a once-in-a-lifetime trip that you want to take. This book is a road map to help you navigate your journey to that place. As with any road map, there are multiple routes to get to a destination, some might take longer than others, while some might be more direct, but more challenging because of obstacles in your path (e.g., hills, traffic, steep mountains). We want you to see your journey as a process within your control, in which you decide how to proceed. As in any lengthy journey, you might want to get to the destination as soon as possible, but fatigue may set in and require some adjustments. There may be times when you change course due to adverse conditions or unforeseen obstacles that appear along the way.

This workbook is designed to be a comprehensive guide to managing BFRBs of all kinds. It provides information to help you understand BFRBs and how they work, as well as many exercises which we are calling *action items*, to help you with a multitude of different aspects of recovery. It is highly recommended that you engage in the **action items** that are presented to help you get the most out of this workbook. Simply reading about the **action items**, but not doing them, is like reading about healthy eating and exercise, without actually changing your diet and activity level. The targeted changes that you make along the way, consistently and carefully, will help ensure that you ultimately accomplish your goals. The key to improvement and actual, lasting behavior change is to commit to the process in a thoughtful and meaningful way. Know that this journey is not an easy one, and you will face many challenges along the way that can undermine confidence and threaten success. However, overcoming obstacles and setbacks fosters resilience and well-earned confidence and satisfaction. Approach this journey with an open heart and fire in your belly. While it is not an easy path, it is one worth facing bravely.

Overview of the Chapters

This workbook is divided into three parts. Part I (Chapters 1–3) focuses on preparation, including an emphasis on awareness of the obvious components of your BFRB as well as the more subtle ones. Part II (Chapters 4–8) focuses on specific, individualized interventions designed to help you reduce your BFRB and to provide you with guidance on how to address BFRBs from a broader, holistic perspective. Part III (Chapters 9–10) focuses on important lifestyle changes and successful maintenance of your recovery for the long haul.

Part I Preparation and Gaining Awareness of Your BFRB

Following this introduction, the remainder of Chapter 1 provides useful information about BFRBs: What are they? Why do people pull hair and pick skin? How many people have a BFRB? This information will help you better understand your BFRB and will set the stage for your effort using the Comprehensive Behavioral (ComB) approach. This chapter will also address the personal toll of your BFRB, including the shame and negative self-concept that often accompanies these behaviors. **Action items** are aimed at preparing you for the journey ahead. We have found that preparation is, in many ways, the most important part of this process and one that is often overlooked. Consider packing for a trip. You would likely spend some time in preparation by gathering information about the weather and envisioning activities you plan to do when you arrive at your destination. Only after some careful preparation are you able to pack the right clothing and supplies to make the trip enjoyable and successful. In similar ways, we are going to help you gather the information needed to create a packing list, which will make your journey toward recovery both empowering and effective. Chapter 2 will focus on the ComB approach by describing how relevant information about BFRBs are organized into categories or "domains," and the ways that a number of factors within these domains function to keep your BFRB active and strong. You will identify which domains impact your BFRB and you will understand how important these domains are in promoting BFRB activity. Think of this chapter as your travel plan. Where do you want to go and what do you need to know to get there? Chapter 3 will describe how, believe it or not, your BFRB has understandable functions that it serves in your life. Identifying these functions are important steps as you prepare your trip itinerary. We will also address common roadblocks or diversions that you may encounter as you move forward, as well as how to solve them.

Part II Interventions and Skill Building: Selecting and Using Interventions

Chapters 4 through 8 will describe each of the BFRB domains separately, help you to decide which ones are relevant to you, and give you specific tools from each domain to navigate your BFRB. The five domains by chapter are: 4 Sensory, 5 Cognitive, 6 Affective, 7 Motor, and 8 Place. It may help you to remember the domains with the acronym *SCAMP*.

> **S**ensory: sensations that either cause or are satisfied by the BFRB
> **C**ognitive: thoughts or beliefs that either cause or are satisfied by the BFRB
> **A**ffective: emotions that either cause or are satisfied by the BFRB
> **M**otor: movements or postures that facilitate the BFRB, as well as awareness of the BFRB
> **P**lace: environmental cues and external triggers for the BFRB

Part III Lifestyle Changes and Maintenance of Recovery

Chapter 9 will focus on the positive impact of self-care on BFRBs specifically, as well as on other important aspects of your life. We will suggest an array of self-care strategies that can make for a more enjoyable and successful journey. Chapter 10 is dedicated to helping you maintain gains and prevent slips and relapse for the long haul.

Getting Started

Before delving into "what works," we find that laying the groundwork for change is an important first step. What does this mean? Well, it means a couple of things including providing accurate and detailed information about what BFRBs are, and dispelling some of the common myths that can lead to misunderstandings and confusion about the true nature of BFRBs.

What You Need to Know

BFRBs Defined

So, what do we know about BFRBs? Body focused repetitive behaviors are actions directed toward one's own body that cause damage to the body's integrity and, when done to an extreme, can cause physical, emotional, social, and psychological problems. BFRBs include, but are not limited to:

- hair pulling disorder (also known as trichotillomania)
- skin picking disorder (also known as excoriation disorder or dermatillomania), including picking of blemishes, scabs, calluses, and so on
- onychophagia (compulsive nail biting)
- compulsive nose picking
- compulsive biting the inside of the cheek or tongue
- lip biting or picking
- nail/cuticle picking and biting

In the *Diagnostic and Statistical Manual of Mental Disorders* (DSM), fifth edition TR (2022), both hair pulling disorder (HPD) and skin picking disorder (SPD) are included as Obsessive Compulsive and Related Disorders (OCD) and the others are subsumed under the umbrella of Other Obsessive Compulsive and Related Disorders. To be clear, BFRBs are not a form of OCD, but they are classified in the category of OCD and related disorders. Think of them as a distant cousin of OCD. We prefer the term HPD to the more scientific term, trichotillomania, and SPD to the alternatives, excoriation disorder and the older term dermatillomania, and we will use them throughout this workbook. The techniques described in this workbook are appropriate for all types of BFRBs with minor adjustments to fit specific needs.

Genetic Basis

Although research examining the heritability of HPD and SPD is barely underway, there is some preliminary evidence suggesting that BFRBs have a genetic component. For example, researchers reported the incidence of HPD in first-degree family members of subjects with HPD as 10 percent, while it was just 1–2 percent in first-degree relatives of those without HPD. In addition, rates of skin picking and other BFRBs tend to be higher in relatives of people with HPD (Keuthen et al., 2014). Thus, even if a person with HPD does not have a family member who pulls hair, they are more likely to have someone in their family who bites nails, picks cuticles, bites lips or cheeks, or picks at acne or scabs than chance alone would allow. For now, we can say with some certainty that BFRBs tend to run in families. Why is this important? Because people tend to want to blame their environment for their condition, for example, "Hair pulling is the result of bad parenting or a negative event that occurred." For the most part we know that regardless of the goodness of parenting or the degree of negative life events, hair pulling and skin picking behaviors are likely facilitated by genetics. Now that does not mean that people who experience negative life events, such as chaotic family lives or early trauma, will not have a BFRB, but we believe that the genetic predisposition was already there. Perhaps the negative life event "awakened" the BFRB which otherwise might not have manifested itself. However, we do see many people with a BFRB who report having lovely, happy, uneventful childhoods, free of trauma or serious adversity.

Age of Onset and Symptom Development

The average age of onset for BFRBs is around twelve years old, although these behaviors can begin as early as infancy or much deeper into adulthood. It is not known if this onset is related to puberty itself and the hormonal changes associated with this period of extensive transformation or whether other factors influence this typical age of onset. Perhaps the emotional turmoil that is common in early teen years may play some role in triggering these symptoms. For people who report a later onset, perhaps in their twenties or thirties, many report having experienced other BFRBs earlier in their lives. For example, a woman whose hair pulling began when she was thirty-five years old may also report that in her early adolescence, she bit her nails and picked at her cuticles. So, although the hair pulling did not start until adulthood, her history with BFRBs actually began in early adolescence, which is consistent with current understanding of BFRB onset. Think about your BFRB, have you ever had one of the other varieties and has it changed over time into another form?

Co-occurring Conditions

Research suggests that depression and anxiety commonly coexist with BFRBs. What we are not always sure of is whether these are contributing causes of BFRBs or whether they are the effects of years of dealing with them. Does your BFRB cause you to be depressed or anxious, or do sadness and anxiety link with your BFRB in some other ways? If feelings of sadness or anxiety impact you more profoundly than your BFRB or if they predated onset of your BFRB, you might consider addressing those other conditions first before you tackle your BFRB. As we will emphasize throughout this workbook, addressing your BFRB will take energy and time. If you are struggling emotionally, to the point that those feelings take up much of your energy and focus, it makes sense to deal with them as a priority, then return to your BFRB when you are feeling better and up to the challenge. This might look like engaging in individual therapy focused on addressing any symptoms of depression, anxiety, or unattended-to trauma from the past. While this is not imperative, it can be helpful to give you the best chance for success along this journey.

Prevalence

The prevalence of HPD in adults has been estimated to be as low as 2 percent and as high as 5 percent. However, small sample sizes, varied inclusion criteria, and other factors may account for the discrepancies (Mansueto &

Rogers, 2012). For SPD, reported prevalence rates have an even wider range in various studies, but overall, an incidence of about 5 percent in the general population seems plausible (Odlaug & Grant, 2012). Because individuals with these disorders often conceal them from others, it is possible that BFRBs may be underreported in the general population. What seems certain is that BFRBs are *far more common* than was thought only decades ago and that prevalence rates are similar to those of OCD and other anxiety disorders. What this means is that you are not alone – there are millions of other people out there who pull and pick, just like you. One of the hallmark experiences of individuals with BFRBs is how alone they feel. We are here to tell you that you are not, in fact, alone and, to the contrary, these problems are actually quite common.

What We Do Not Know

Although we believe that BFRBs likely have a genetic contribution, that they probably affect more women than men (although this is debatable as it may be that more women seek treatment while an equal number of men are actually struggling with a BFRB), and that these conditions seem to affect up to 5 percent of the population, the truth is that there is a great deal of uncertainty about even those fundamental points. We do not know, for example, whether or not early childhood pulling and picking is a precursor to the disorder that presents in adolescence or adulthood, or whether it is a self-limiting aspect in the normal development of some infants. Further, we do not know the biochemical underpinnings of BFRBs or of any psychotropic medications that reliably help people who suffer with them. We do not know the relationships that BFRBs have to other psychiatric disorders, or even if there are relationships. We do not know what specific neurological pathways or brain circuitry are involved in BFRBs. These and others are important questions that remain largely unanswered and therefore warrant further research efforts, some of which are underway. Rather than be dismayed by this state of affairs however, it is useful to consider that the scientific investigation of BFRBs is relatively new when compared with most other recognized psychological disorders, and that what we *have* learned about them in the past three decades has provided us with a solid foundation for helping those who suffer their effects.

How Do BFRBs Begin?

Body focused repetitive behaviors typically begin in adolescence and often they first appear in seemingly benign circumstances that can set off a potentially lifelong problem. Most individuals report that they accidently "discovered" the effects of BFRB activities during unremarkable moments when their fingers explored their hair or skin. For some, it seems as if ordinary grooming of hair and skin went terribly awry. For many teenagers squeezing pimples is virtually a rite of passage, but among a minority of these, squeezing and picking at blemishes goes far beyond grooming and becomes the focus of much of their distress in life.

Yet BFRBs can begin in a multitude of other ways as well. One adult client who pulled out her eyelashes reported that as a child she had heard that wishes will come true if you pull out an eyelash while making the wish. She quickly realized that it didn't work in the way she hoped it would, but the "special feeling" she experienced at that first pull led her to continue the practice for over a decade. Another client's HPD started when she pulled a hair from her scalp to view under a microscope for a high school biology class. These behaviors likely persisted because of a genetic vulnerability interacting with contributing life experiences. In other cases, people reported that they either observed someone else pulling or picking or heard that others did those things, became curious, and tried it themselves. Unfortunately, over time those activities became uncontrollable and hard to stop. It is clear that there is a great deal of variety in the experiences associated with how skin picking and hair pulling initially begin and each person will have a unique story to tell. Regardless of the origin of the behavior for any individual, BFRB practices can become so interwoven with the fabric of one's life that they feel as natural, automatic, and pervasive as moving one's body.

What Are the Secondary Physical, Emotional, and Social Effects of BFRBs?

Listening to individuals with BFRBs describe their experiences provides us with opportunities to understand the deep hurt, damaged relationships, lost opportunities, and other negative impacts on their quality of life, whether as an adult or as a young person who bears this burden. Consistently, people with BFRBs report experiencing a life marred by shame, embarrassment, and isolation as a result of the BFRB. People often wonder "Why me?" "Am I the only one?" or "What is wrong with me?" In addition to the obvious, physical impacts of BFRBs, many report negative effects on their educational or career pursuits, while others report family conflict and other interpersonal problems stemming from their BFRB (Woods et al., 2006). Research often does not include these nearly universal emotional and interpersonal symptoms of BFRBs, but treatment cannot ignore those factors and, as a result, they will be addressed directly in this workbook.

Many people with BFRBs carry a profound degree of shame, often compounded by a history of feeling blamed and experiencing social rejection, teasing, nagging, and isolation from others. Sometimes parents do not understand these behaviors and, with good intentions, may get upset or punish their child for pulling or picking. Peers may tease, say unkind things, or be downright abusive and, as a result, people may pull away from others to avoid teasing or negative comments. All of these negative responses from others can cause a person to feel different or somehow broken. In addition, shame also arises because of the self-inflicted nature of BFRBs and the physical damage that is potentially observable to others. This combination of ingredients can take huge personal and interpersonal tolls. Self-imposed social isolation and avoidance of day-to-day life experiences and relationships with others is common for people who strive to hide their BFRB from others, sometimes even from those closest to them. People with BFRBs often fear that they will be judged harshly for their behavior, and some may have actually experienced hurtful reactions from others. In severe cases, people may choose to avoid many social opportunities and intimate relationships to keep their secret safely hidden (Stemberger et al., 2000). Others spend so much time engaging in their BFRB (or in the activities needed to cover up the damage caused by it), that it prevents them from spending that time with the people they love. Think for a minute about the many ways your BFRB(s) have impacted you over the years (action item 1.1).

Identify the various ways your BFRB(s) has had an impact on your life

How has your BFRB(s) impacted you? Check off any ways that you or your life have been impacted by the results of your BFRB. Add any impacts that may not be listed here.

Physical:

- ☐ hair loss
- ☐ baldness
- ☐ uneven hair line
- ☐ hair not regrowing
- ☐ scarring
- ☐ frequent scabs
- ☐ discoloration of the skin
- ☐ other: _____

Medical:

- ☐ infections
- ☐ stomach problems, excessive stomach pain, gas, bloating, hair in stool or trichobezoars (i.e., hair that accumulates in the stomach or intestine that sometimes requires surgical intervention)
- ☐ repetitive movement problems, carpel tunnel syndrome
- ☐ dental problems
- ☐ alopecia
- ☐ permanent damage to the body, deformities
- ☐ loss of fingernails/toenails
- ☐ need for surgery or other medical procedures
- ☐ avoidance of medical exams
- ☐ eye problems as a result of lash pulling
- ☐ other: _____

Social:

- ☐ avoidance of social activities where BFRB damage might be revealed (e.g., swimming, wearing shorts/bathing suits, windy environment)
- ☐ avoidance of romantic relationships
- ☐ interference with friendships
- ☐ problematic behavioral/emotional displays in adolescence/childhood
- ☐ family conflicts
- ☐ social isolation
- ☐ time spent engaging in the BFRB interferes with social time
- ☐ other: _____

Academic:

- ☐ lower grades (due to distraction or time spent engaging in a BFRB and not studying)
- ☐ reduced academic expectations for oneself or by others
- ☐ avoidance of higher education
- ☐ other: _____

Emotional/Psychological:

- ☐ feelings of shame
- ☐ feelings of isolation
- ☐ negative reactions of others
- ☐ being bullied
- ☐ low self-esteem/self-concept

ACTION ITEM 1.1

- ☐ feeling blamed for the BFRB
- ☐ feelings of sadness
- ☐ feelings of guilt
- ☐ anger at oneself for the BFRB
- ☐ other: _____

Financial:

- ☐ money spent on wigs, doctors, treatments, and so on
- ☐ loss of time that could have been spent working
- ☐ loss of a job
- ☐ avoidance of seeking a job due to fear of being found out
- ☐ avoiding work
- ☐ other: _____

What feelings arise as you take note of the ways your BFRB has impacted you? It is important to understand the wider effects of your BFRB because taking stock of these can help to increase your motivation to change your behavior – that is the goal.

Addressing Shame

Shame is perhaps the most profound emotion associated with BFRBs and is experienced almost universally by people who struggle with these disorders. We have found that it is important to address feelings of shame early on in efforts to overcome BFRBs, to promote greater success on a multitude of levels. The following exercise will help you to identify your "BFRB story" and begin the process of undoing shame about your BFRB. In order to recover from the impact of challenging events in life, it helps to put words to them (action item 1.2).

ACTION ITEM 1.2

Capture your "BFRB story" in your own words as a step toward reducing shame and increasing empowerment

Write a story about your journey with your BFRB. How did it begin? How has it changed over the course of your life? In other words, if you were telling a close friend about your experience living with a BFRB, how would you tell that story?

_____
_____
_____
_____
_____
_____
_____
_____
_____
_____
_____
_____
_____
_____
_____
_____
_____
_____
_____
_____
_____
_____
_____
_____
_____
_____
_____
_____
_____
_____

What feelings did you experience when writing your story? What is the story that you tell yourself regarding your BFRB? What story do you tell others? Is your narrative accurate and helpful? Are there words in your story that are negative or judgmental such as "hate," "failure," or "ugly?"

Now, if you were to write the "rest of the story," what would it be and how would it end? Take a moment to think about what a reasonable path to recovery would look like, where would your story go from here? Imagine yourself walking down the beach wearing whatever you want, with no care about covering up a bald spot or scars from picking. What are your dreams, your fantasies about what life with a managed BFRB would be? It's tempting to wish to simply stop pulling or picking and never give it a second thought. However, that wish may be a bit unrealistic given that this has been a part of your life for as long as it has. Would it be possible to reduce the behavior, the urge, or both? What might managing your behavior look like? What could you do then that you cannot or will not do now? Do you have any beliefs about whether or not this is possible? It is possible! Think about what the ending to your story might be (action item 1.3).

ACTION ITEM 1.3

Envision the end of your story

This exercise should help you to clarify your goals – what would be different if you were successful? Try to refrain from using black and white language such as "I will stop completely" or "I will never pick again." Instead consider "If I have an urge or I do pick, I know what I need to do" or "When there is a big change or transition in my life, I will take these steps proactively to help myself with my BFRB." Write your idea of what the next few weeks, months, and years might look like, if things were to go well during this process. Think about how your story will end – how do you want it to end? What activities will you be able to do? Remember to be realistic and specific in your responses.

How was that? Were you surprised at how you want your story to end? When you think about your story ending in this way, how does it make you feel?

Why Do People Engage in BFRBs, and Why Do You?

Understanding why you engage in a BFRB is fundamental for recovery from your BFRB. The short answer though is simple – because it feels right to do it. You engage in your BFRB because it helps you in some way to get your needs met. In other words, it is *functional.* How does your BFRB work for you? How would you feel if you suddenly were not able to pull or pick? As humans, at times we engage in behaviors that are not good for us, even when we are aware that we are engaging in them. For example, people might be aware that they are eating a certain food that is not a "great choice" for them (e.g., a hamburger and french fries, chocolate cake, potato chips, etc.), especially if they are trying to eat healthfully – but they eat it anyway. We have all make poor food choices because in that moment, the moment when considering the options, we choose what we *want, not what's best for us*, because experiences lead us to believe that it will satisfy us to do so. There are probably times when you are well aware that you want to pull or pick, and you know that you probably "should not," but you do it anyway. Why is this? As humans, we are constantly in the service of our own satisfaction and pleasure, even when that pleasure comes at a cost to our long-term goals or desires.

Despite the reality that hair pulling and skin picking lead to unwanted and sometimes awful outcomes, at the same time they provide some comfort or benefit in the moment they occur. Most people with BFRBs report that they feel guilty, angry, frustrated, or sad after an episode of pulling or picking – is this true for you? Such feelings can lead to self-recrimination and feelings of worthlessness, powerlessness, and even self-loathing. When short-term results are positive, behavior is very reinforcing, even when the long-term results are negative. If hangovers occurred the minute a person had a sip of alcohol, few people would likely drink. The short-term rewards for drinking alcohol override the negative effects that come later, up to a point. BFRBs work the same way. These short-term desirable effects of BFRBs are what is reinforcing, even if they are fleeting. The long-term results are negative and could possibly even lead to more pulling and picking. A powerful way to change this "short-term versus long-term gratification cycle" is to learn to respond to yourself with tenderness and compassion – to talk to yourself like you would talk to your best friend or some other loved one. Self-compassion is not simply telling yourself "You are great!" or "Your BFRB is no big deal," but something much more profound. Self-compassion is not self-reassurance or denial, but kind words when you are suffering (e.g., facing an urge to pull or pick). Self-compassion is meeting yourself with tenderness and love, without judgment or harsh words. We will talk more deeply about self-compassion in Chapter 9, but for now, try this next exercise to get a feel for what self-compassion would look like for you (action item 1.4).

Identify and heal negativity by encouraging you to develop more compassion for yourself – exploring "best friend thoughts"

Imagine that your best friend, someone you feel very close to, had the exact BFRB problem that you have. How would you speak to this person? What would you say to them in difficult situations?

Situation 1: What would you say to them when they wanted to pull/pick?

Example: This must be so hard. I am so sorry that you are going through this. What can I do to help?

_____
_____
_____
_____

Situation 2: What would you say to them when they had just had a pulling/picking episode and they were feeling bad about it?

Example: I know this is hard, but you can get back on track. Everyone disappoints themselves at times. You are no different from the rest of us.

_____
_____
_____
_____

Situation 3: What would you say to someone who was upset about their appearance and did not want to go out?

Example: You are a beautiful person! Having sores or bald spots doesn't change that.

_____
_____
_____
_____

Situation 4: What would you say to a friend who feels frustrated with the thoughtless things some people say about their BFRB?

Example: These people have no idea about what it's really like having a BFRB.

_____
_____
_____
_____

ACTION ITEM 1.4

Situation 5: What would you say to a friend who just had a big pulling/picking setback?

Example: *Oh honey, this is so hard! I am so sorry that you are struggling, and I am here for you.*

_____
_____
_____
_____

How did that feel? Did it feel weird or fake to think about saying supportive words to yourself? If so, this is completely normal. It is important to try it anyway. Even when it feels like you are lying to yourself, practice using "best friend thoughts" until they start to feel normal and natural.

A Word About Urges

Throughout this book we will refer to sensations that encourage you to engage in your BFRB as "urges." What really are urges though? The word 'urge' is often defined as a strong desire or impulse. When we refer to urges, we are talking about a variety of experiences that may be described differently by different people. Some people describe an urge as a sensation on the skin, while others describe them as more emotionally based. Still other people describe urges as more cognitively based, rather than physically. Regardless of how you experience urges, we know that for many people the feeling of an urge is tremendously powerful and can seem impossible to tolerate without performing some action to reduce it. We will address the concept of urges throughout this workbook and, with time, you will learn to respond differently to them. While we cannot reduce or eliminate urges for you, we can teach you how to respond to them utilizing tools to help you take care of yourself in those moments of suffering. Next, we thought it might be helpful to dispel some common misunderstandings about BFRBs.

Myths and Misconceptions About BFRBs

Myth 1: *BFRBs are the result of childhood sexual abuse or some other traumatic event.* One common misconception is that BFRBs are the result of prior childhood sexual abuse. This belief is probably based on some early speculation in the professional literature in the absence of reliable data. In reality, there is little to suggest that BFRB sufferers have experienced any more childhood sexual abuse than that found in the general population (Lochner, 2002). Furthermore, only about half of people with a BFRB report any notable life stressors occurring just before or at the time their BFRB started. When such stressors are reported, they tend to be more typical life events such as family stress, the death of a pet, or changing schools. As stated earlier in this chapter, there is little evidence that traumatic events consistently preceded or have a direct impact in causing these disorders, because they most likely result from an interaction between biological factors and varieties of life experiences, most of which are not traumatic. Many people with a BFRB report *no* history of significant trauma at all. That is not to say that a person with a BFRB could not have experienced significant traumatic events in their life, because sometimes they have, and we do not want in any way to discount these painful events. What we are saying is simply that trauma is not the usual cause of BFRBs, nor is it essential for the development of these problems. The truth is negative events such as trauma can bring about a host of psychological disruptions and can make already existing problems even worse. If trauma is something that you struggle with, you might consider addressing that experience in therapy with an appropriately trained clinician which would help to set a firm foundation for progress in overcoming your BFRB.

Myth 2: *BFRBs are the result of some underlying issue that needs to be resolved, because once the "root cause" of the hair pulling or skin picking is uncovered and addressed, the behavior will disappear.* This misconception is, in part, born out of psychodynamic perspectives and will likely lead people with a BFRB toward frustration. This idea that a BFRB is a sign of some deeper disturbance or a symptom of some hidden conflict, implies that a person has more serious issues to resolve. This is not true in the vast majority of cases, and this assumption can cause people to believe that there is something inherently wrong with them. Many people with a BFRB have no more deeper issues to resolve than any other person apart from their BFRB. Put simply, there is no compelling empirical basis to support the view that therapy focused on gaining insight into otherwise unresolved, underlying issues has any impact on helping to mitigate BFRBs.

Myth 3: *BFRBs are a form of intentional self-harm or a desire to be unattractive.* While on the surface it may look like the systematic removal of one's hair (particularly in more severe cases) is a form of self-mutilation, or that creating lesions in one's skin is a form of self-harm akin to self-inflicted cutting or burning of the skin, this is simply not the case. People with BFRBs pull their hair and pick their skin because it helps to achieve some desirable outcome, but self-damage is not typically the objective. The driving force for the BFRB is not "to destroy myself" or "to be unattractive," but rather to somehow "feel better." We find it more helpful to view BFRBs as ways to self-regulate, whether it be emotional, sensory, physical, neurological, or otherwise. We will talk more about these important factors in Chapters 4–8, but for now know that BFRBs help you to self-regulate, not self-mutilate. We will discuss self-regulation more in Chapter 9, but for now know that BFRBs are often a way for you to regulate some aspect of your experience, to improve whatever it is that you are experiencing.

Myth 4: *Willpower is the key to success in ending a BFRB.* This widely held belief holds that hair pulling and skin picking are mere habits that can easily be changed if a person has the desire and/or willpower to do so. Quite the contrary! BFRBs are more accurately viewed as strongly ingrained, complex phenomena resulting from a mixture of psychological and neurological factors. Over time, BFRBs become associated with a variety of triggers and reinforcing sensations that encourage their continuation. Assuming that BFRBs are "simply habits" implies that they are easily changed by trying harder. Such assumptions often result in frustration and self-blame when change does not happen easily or reliably. Not only are BFRBs not easily changed, but they are also typically accompanied by ambivalence – a feeling of wanting to stop but still driven to pull or pick. In fact, ambivalence about giving up a BFRB tends to be the rule with very few exceptions and is *not* an indication of the potential or lack of potential for change. Remember that hair pulling and skin picking can provide a wide range of positive experiences for you, ones that might be difficult to give up. Mixed feelings about giving up these satisfying but unhealthy experiences, despite their negative, longer-term consequences, is a challenge for every human being and it certainly is not unique to you.

Readiness for Change: Motivation versus Readiness

Did you know that you can want to change your behaviors, but not yet be ready to take steps to accomplish that? Have you ever committed yourself to getting more exercise, signed up for a gym membership, or bought some athletic equipment and found that you were still unable to reach your goals? Most people have had the common experience of *wanting* something to change, but for whatever reason not taking the necessary steps to make change happen. Because you are reading this workbook, we can assume that you *want* to change your behavior, you *are* motivated, but it is possible that you are not yet ready to do the things necessary to achieve your goals. However, maybe you *are* at a place of readiness, and you are perfectly poised to take the necessary steps to change.

Assess your readiness for the effort required to overcome your BFRB

The Scales of Readiness

List on either side of the scale your reasons to or not to work on changing your BFRB. For example, "It will take too much effort," or "I don't have the time" might be reasons not to work toward change, whereas "I would be able to enjoy not wearing a wig" or "I would feel so much more confident" might be reasons to work toward change. Be honest as it only helps you to identify any ambivalence early on in this process.

Reasons to change my BFRB:	Reasons not to change my BFRB:

Which side of your scale is more heavily weighted? What does this suggest about your readiness to change? Have you been completely honest about what you might miss if you stopped engaging in your BFRB? If not, go back and modify your responses. Use this exercise to help you identify things that might get in the way of your progress, things that you are reluctant to give up, and therefore might hold you back. Behavior change is *hard,* and we forget that often we have good reasons for continuing our problem behaviors. In working through this book, we will ask you to do hard things – we will ask you to forgo your BFRB for other behaviors. This is going to be hard! We want you to be prepared to do hard things, because it is worth it to do them. Anything done in life that is worthwhile was likely hard to achieve and often includes forward and backward movement in the process. It is important to address any roadblocks now, as well as along the way, so that they do not become obstacles that could deter you from success in your BFRB journey.

One important point to keep in mind is that ambivalence is normal, expected, and can be overcome. This means that your responses to the "Scales of Readiness" exercise (action item 1.5) are expected to show some level of ambivalence about change. In order to make changes, you need to be aware of your ambivalence and be committed to accomplishing your goals. Identifying obstacles and effectively addressing them are necessary steps toward successful completion of your journey. How do you address ambivalence? The answer is through problem-solving. For example, if one of your "reasons not to change my BFRB" is that "it helps me to relax after a long day," you would want to find some other methods for relaxation in the evening hours. Review your list of "reasons not to change" and begin to problem-solve how to address these issues.

Expectations and Goal Setting

It is time to think about setting some goals for your journey's end. Many people will say that their goal is to never pick or pull again. This type of "all or nothing" goal can pose some problems that we should look at closely. If I set a goal of "never eating junk food again," I will, at some point in my life, fail. So, we do not want you to set yourself up for failure, we want you to set yourself up for success. We know that slips are inevitable and will happen, what we do not want is for that slip (pulling ten hairs) to turn into a complete relapse (pulling 500 hairs because those ten hairs represented a complete failure). Outside of an episode one can see that pulling ten hairs is much less of a setback than pulling 500 hairs, but in that moment, when frustration and self-condemnation set in, one can feel defeated and like giving up. You must remember that *slips happen* and can be managed through problem-solving and good judgment, to prevent the slip from becoming a total relapse.

In our clinical work, we have seen that setting realistic, manageable goals that focus on "doing" rather than "not doing" is a productive and ultimately more successful approach than "all or nothing" goals. Consider the junk food example, a better goal would be: "I will eat 4 servings of fruits and vegetables a day." This is a "doing" goal and though it might not be the complete answer, it will be a step toward having a healthier diet and limiting intake of junk food. An example that relates to BFRBs might be setting a goal of "taking my toothbrush to the kitchen sink to brush my teeth (doing), as opposed to "not picking in the bathroom after having brushed my teeth (not doing)" (action item 1.6).

Set realistic and achievable goals to keep you on the road to success

Check all that apply to you and your life.

- ☐ I would like to go places and not worry about hiding my BFRB.
- ☐ I would like to grow my hair back to the point that I do not worry about people noticing.
- ☐ I would like to allow my skin to heal and stay healed.
- ☐ I would like to pull/pick so minimally that it does not bother me at all.
- ☐ I would like to love myself, even though I have a BFRB.
- ☐ I would like to feel good about myself.
- ☐ I would like to view my BFRB as a small part of who I am, not my sole identity.
- ☐ I would like to accept myself as I am.
- ☐ I would like to be able to talk about my BFRB without feeling ashamed.
- ☐ I would like to be able to participate in activities like swimming, wearing shorts/bathing suits, going out on a windy day, and so on, without worrying about people noticing.
- ☐ I would like to see myself as a healed person, not a broken one.
- ☐ I would like to have more time in my life to do what I love to do.
- ☐ I would like to save money that I spend on my BFRB or spend it on other things.
- ☐ I would like to feel confident in my success and in my life.
- ☐ I would like to accept myself as I am, a nonperfect person who is doing their best.
- ☐ I would like to get curious about my BFRB and be interested rather than ashamed of it.
- ☐ I would like to be compassionate about lapses and know that a lapse is not a failure, but just a bump along the road.
- ☐ I would like to "live well" with my BFRB, potentially using what I learn to help others feel less shame.
- ☐ I would like to _____
- ☐ I would like to _____
- ☐ I would like to _____
- ☐ I would like to _____
- ☐ I would like to _____
- ☐ I would like to _____

Do you notice how goals can be about improving your *life*, not just about reducing, or managing your BFRB? Return to this page frequently to add more goals as they develop. In fact, you might add your goals on your smart phone home page, tape them to your bathroom mirror, or place them in some other spot that you look at frequently. You will want to keep your goals in mind throughout this process. If, when traveling to an unfamiliar city you desire to see the local attractions, you would want to keep that goal front and center so that other distractions do not keep you from missing out on that. Keeping your goals realistic, positive, and in the forefront is an important part of staying on course. Think about all of the things that you would like to be doing instead of engaging in your BFRB – spending time with loved ones, exercising, engaging in hobbies, learning something new, doing things that you typically avoid due to your BFRB. Remember to add these things to your goals list to help see the *value* in changing your behavior. We want you to see that managing your BFRB is not about taking away the thing you enjoy but rather opens up so many things for you in your future. Reducing your BFRB actually *increases* your options in life.

Behavior Change Is Not a Light Switch

If we could comfortably teleport ourselves to our travel destinations, we would do it, but that is not yet possible. To get to your final destination, you might have to get into a cab to take you to the airport, go through security, wait for your plane, board your plane, fly on the plane, wait for your bags, take a train to a town, and possibly partake of more steps! Any journey has a series of important requirements along the way, and no trip is perfect. You might have flight delays due to weather, cabs get stuck in traffic, flights get cancelled, all of which are beyond your control. More than likely, there will be hitches along the way on this BFRB journey. The goal is to be as flexible as possible and to tolerate any unfortunate frustrations with grace and acceptance, as well as the resolve to keep moving forward. Developing better coping skills to manage these inevitable "hiccups" along the way is key. Recognize that most hitches are beyond our control, but a part of the change process. When flights get cancelled it makes little sense to spend all of your time bemoaning how upset you are that the flight was cancelled, and more sense to work toward rerouting yourself on another flight or finding something fun to do while you are delayed. For example, I might leave for the airport with plenty of time, but a traffic accident that slows me down is far beyond my control. Getting mad at the people who caused the accident does not allow me to move any faster, it just adds to my frustration. Using that time to breathe and listen to a favorite playlist or podcast is a better use of time. Know that there will be setbacks along the way on this journey, and that is normal and expected. In fact, it would be miraculous if you did not experience some setbacks in your BFRB journey. Setbacks might occur where you struggle with recurring urges or succumb to a disheartening episode of BFRB activity after doing well for some period of time. A setback might occur after some identifiable stressor that is beyond your control, or lapses may happen seemingly for no reason at all. The important thing is to predict that setbacks *will* occur. Be prepared for them, and *do not judge yourself harshly* when they occur. The absolute best thing that you can do when a setback occurs is to *learn from it* and use that information in the future. Be prepared to ask yourself "What could I have done differently instead of pulling/picking?" or "How could I have managed that situation more effectively, knowing what I now know?" Use your "best friend" thinking when dealing with setbacks to avoid negative self-talk and harsh emotions. You have to be your own cheerleader through this process.

Timing Is Everything

One thing that can make it difficult to manage a BFRB, even when motivation and readiness are there, is poor timing. For example, few people would be likely to plan a hiking trip during their recovery from major foot surgery. This would not be the best timing for the trip. With this in mind, make sure that now is a good time to focus on your BFRB. Changing a well-entrenched behavior, no matter what it is, takes time and effort each day to be successful. Attempting this at a time when there is too much on your plate or you are under a great deal of stress will only cause you to feel like a failure, to feel defeated. We do not want you to feel defeated, we want you to feel empowered – we want you to be successful on your journey! We also understand that this is your journey, and you should ultimately make the decision about what is best for you. We are just asking you to evaluate what is on your plate right now and to think about whether or not you currently have the bandwidth to take on this challenge. Doing this exercise might cause you to set some limits in areas of your life to free up some space for this work as well (action item 1.7).

ACTION ITEM 1.7

Determine if now is a good time to start your journey, or if staying in preparation for a little while longer makes sense, until the time is right

Take a minute to take stock of all of the obligations you have in your life right now. We will break them down into categories to help you think about how much mental and emotional energy you have available to you for your journey. Just like taking a trip, you want, if possible, to be rested and ready for travel. No trip is easy if you begin tired and overwhelmed. As fun as travel is, it can also be tiring. Below you will find scales that will help you to rate your stress in different areas of your life. "Work" might be a big project that you just took on, "School" might involve academic stress, "Family" might be marital stress or having young children, "Social" might be interpersonal distress with a friend, and "Emotional" might be a co-occurring disorder such as depression or anxiety. Rate each area of your life from 0–5 and then add up your scores to get a total from 0–25. If you scored above a 16, perhaps consider waiting until things have calmed down. Again, this is completely up to you. In the meantime, you could focus your efforts on self-care and self-compassion (see Chapter 9), to help better prepare you for this journey. If you have a great deal of stress in your life *and* you still want to embark on this journey, that is okay too. Please understand that we are only trying to help you see what challenges lie ahead and to best prepare for them.

	No problem!	Minor	Some stress	Moderate stress	Heavy stress	Severe
Work	0	1	2	3	4	5
School	0	1	2	3	4	5
Family	0	1	2	3	4	5
Social/ relationships	0	1	2	3	4	5
Emotions	0	1	2	3	4	5
Total						

Total: _____

After looking at all of the areas in your life that are needing your attention and your energy, how do you feel about starting this journey now, at this point in time? Are you in a good place in terms of having the time and the mental, physical, and emotional energy to get started? If you are, that is great! If you are not, that is good to know – you may just want to hit the pause button and skip to Chapter 9 where we focus on self-care. A dedicated focus on self-care until the "storm has passed" allows you to be refreshed and prepared for your BFRB journey. For those of you ready to get started, let us think about what your life might be like should you overcome your BFRB.

What Would Life Be like with You Managing Your BFRB?

Just as when you plan a vacation, you will have to plan for the journey ahead. When traveling you will have to answer questions about: Where you will stay? What will you eat? What attractions you will see? Planning your BFRB journey will require similar considerations: How will your life be different without your BFRB? How will you manage your stress? How will you engage in activities of daily life without it? Can you envision yourself as a person who does not engage in their BFRB on a regular basis? What would that person be like? How would they manage situations that typically bring on the BFRB? How would they manage life differently without pulling or picking?

So, at this point, how are you feeling about setting off on your BFRB journey? Are you feeling like now is the right time? Do you feel like you are willing to make changes as well as a willingness to do some hard things and persevere in the process? If so, let us continue on to Chapter 2. If not, we recommend you jump to Chapter 9 and explore self-care now. A focus on addressing your broader personal needs may help you improve your readiness to encourage the many specific changes required to make your amazing journey a successful one. In addition, self-care oftentimes improves self-confidence, happiness, and a general sense of well-being, all of which will serve you well as you embark on this journey.

Chapter Summary and Roadmap

In this chapter you have learned many things about BFRBs, including who has them, what they entail, and the myths and misconceptions about them. You also began to look at your BFRB story – what the story has been in the past and how you want it to end. You also learned how you can be a support to yourself, as you would to a friend. Imagine being that support to yourself by showing yourself understanding, compassion, and encouragement as you might provide to a best friend in need. You set realistic goals, took a look at any ambivalence that you may have about changing your BFRB, and discovered what might hold you back from reaching your goals. Finally, you have looked at timing to determine if now is a good time to approach this important behavior change.

Understand what your BFRB journey will look like

Why I want to change my BFRB:

_____
_____
_____

My goals for this BFRB journey:

_____
_____
_____

Visualizing my life without struggling with my BFRB:

I am _____

I will be able to _____

I will take care of myself by _____

I will let go of _____

I will learn to _____

I will lovingly tell myself that _____

I will support myself by _____

I will show love to myself by _____

Each day I will:

☐ use my "best friend thoughts" when I am struggling

☐ review my reasons to change my BFRB

☐ review my BFRB journey goals

ACTION ITEM 1.8

2

Increasing Awareness of Your BFRB

Overview

In this chapter we focus on the importance of increasing awareness of your BFRB. It should be obvious that it is difficult, if at all possible, to change something you are not consciously aware of. It is common for people with a BFRB to fall into a 'trancelike' state where their mind is completely focused on something else and their awareness of the BFRB is negligible. As important as awareness is, we also know how difficult it can be to focus on the kinds of behaviors that seem easier to ignore. However, this does not help if change is the goal. The most effective way to make a change is to consciously make different choices. For example, if you want to improve your diet, just hoping that that will happen will not be very effective. However, if you buy more vegetables and skip buying the chips when you go grocery shopping, you have made a realistic start toward making better choices. Likewise, we hope to help you make the similar changes with regard to your BFRB. We will provide some new ways to understand your BFRB which, with heightened awareness, will enable you to explore new approaches to gaining greater control. Next, we will teach you about ComB, and how it addresses the many complexities of BFRBs.

Getting Started

The comprehensive behavioral (ComB) model for understanding and treating BFRBs was developed in the early 1990s by Dr. Charles Mansueto and his colleagues at the Behavior Therapy Center of Greater Washington. It all started by spending time with scores of people who were referred by researchers at the National Institute of Health (NIH) who were willing to share their stories. Dr. Mansueto listened carefully, asked many questions about details that had not been explored at the time, and gathered data about hair pulling that led to the development of the ComB conceptualization and treatment models. Based on information collected, Dr. Mansueto saw that these problems were not a simple habit, but were better understood as a set of complex behavioral and psychological features that varied from individual to individual. Further, he realized that the treatments being used at that time for these problems could be improved upon. He believed that treatment required a more comprehensive and individualized approach.

Recognizing the multiple factors that encourage and maintain hair pulling and skin picking, he distilled aspects of the BFRBs into five domains: sensory, cognitive, affective, motor, and place (or, environment), using the acronym SCAMP. Most people's BFRBs have elements that are derived from these five domains. Often these qualities shift from situation to situation and from time to time throughout the day. Understanding your relevant domains helps to point you in the direction of employing effective interventions that are tailored to you and specific to the unique situation you are in at a given time. This chapter will provide an overview of the five SCAMP domains and will help understand which ones pertain to you and your BFRB. We encourage you to return to this chapter over time, adding new information and otherwise updating the information that you record here. This chapter is essential for understanding your BFRB and should be revisited often.

What You Need to Know

Now we will explain the five areas or domains that are relevant to BFRBs. Not everyone experiences all five domains in equal measure, but most people will report that several are particularly relevant to them. After explaining the domains, we can see which ones apply to you with regard to your picking and/or pulling. Please remember that this is important information because understanding these details of your BFRB allows you to select helpful tools that are specific to your needs. Without keen awareness of your familiar behavioral patterns, you will be less able to select the appropriate tools. Understanding when, why, how, where, and during which activities you engage in your BFRB gives you the upper hand in gaining control of them.

One way to think about developing awareness of your BFRB patterns as they pertain to the five SCAMP domains is to get curious about yourself and your BFRB. When we are curious, we are thoughtful and nonjudgmental. Getting curious allows us to really examine what we are experiencing and to open up our minds to a variety of possibilities, rather than making assumptions. Most importantly, getting curious allows us to examine our behavior without judgment, which will begin to alleviate the shame that underlies BFRBs almost universally.

Now, let us talk about the domains. In the following section you will see a general description of each domain. At first, we hope to familiarize you with these new concepts and help you to think about and get curious about your behavior in a new way. Later in the book, Chapters 4 through 8 we will describe each domain in great detail and explore multiple interventions that could be used within each of them. But first, let us get an idea of what these domains look like and how they might relate to you and your BFRB.

The Five SCAMP Domains

Sensory Domain

The first area is the *sensory domain*. From research and decades of clinical experience, we know that BFRBs provide strong sensory experiences that can lead to repeated efforts to recapture those experiences. We all have certain likes and dislikes. If you think about it, you will discover that almost all of your preferences involve sensory experiences. We like how certain things look, feel, sound, smell, or taste. However, it is more complex than that. "*Sensory*" refers not only to the typical senses we think of such as touch, sight, hearing, taste, and smell, but also to how we experience our internal states such as our energy level, temperature, hunger, and how we coordinate activities to achieve desired outcomes. Other notable sensations such as itching, pressure, or tingling might attract you to particular areas of your body from which you are likely to pull or pick. Some people may be less sensitive to bodily sensations than others or prefer greater levels of input and therefore seek out "extra" sensation experiences. For example, some people greatly enjoy the stimulation of a wild amusement park ride, eating hot and spicy food, or going to see a scary movie, rather than spending a quiet day indoors. More sensory-oriented people might have strong preferences for things that feel or look a certain way or that lie within other sensory realms. With regard to BFRBs, these individuals may enjoy the feeling of hairs sliding out of the skin, the feel or look of a pimple "popping," or the removal of rough feeling scabs or out-of-place looking hairs. Additionally, one might enjoy the smell of hair or a scab, biting bits of hair or skin, or even liking a sound that is made when removing an eyelash. Many people are seeking out specific sensations through picking skin or pulling hair, even if they are not consciously aware of it, and there are great individual differences in each person and their preferences. We will explore more about the possible sensations as they relate to BFRBs in Chapter 4.

Cognitive Domain

The *cognitive domain* involves ideas, thoughts, and beliefs. People commonly have thoughts that push them toward pulling or picking. Thoughts might be something like: "These coarse hairs do not belong in my head;" "My pimples will heal better if I get all of the stuff out of them;" or, "I can't concentrate without pulling my hair." Thoughts can also be permission giving, such as "I will just pull out this one hair" or "I deserve this after such a hard day." Other beliefs can lead to more pulling or picking behavior such as "I can't stand having an urge, I have to get rid of it" or "Just one more!" Thoughts can also occur regarding problems that are not directly connected with the BFRB, as when worrying about the future or making difficult or even mundane decisions. Many people report pulling hair or picking skin when they are thinking about problems in their life, worrying about current life issues, or even trying to make a decision that feels weighty. We will talk more about the *cognitive domain* in Chapter 5.

Affective Domain

The *affective domain* refers to emotions that occur before, during, or after a BFRB. Affect is just a technical word for emotion. Many people assume that BFRBs are the result of stress, tension, or anxiety. We do, in fact, see that many people pull or pick when they are feeling nervous or anxious. However, we also see BFRBs occurring frequently in response to other feelings as well. Many people report pulling or picking when they are bored, happy, excited, sad, angry, or frustrated. Sometimes people pull or pick in hopes that they will lessen unwanted emotions during or after pulling or picking. However, it is important to recognize that some people report no emotions at all before, during, or after pulling or picking. We will determine what emotions might be relevant in the case of your BFRB that might otherwise instigate or help perpetuate your BFRB. Then, in Chapter 6, we will identify helpful ways to address these relevant emotions.

Motor Domain

The fourth domain is the *motor domain*, and "motor" refers to body movements and postures that occur while engaging in your BFRB. Sometimes these movements are outside of your awareness but nonetheless, they may lead to pulling or picking. At other times, your body posture might facilitate performance of your BFRB when you position yourself where you can comfortably access your skin or hair. Hands can seem like they have minds of their own when engagement in the BFRB occurs almost unconsciously. In this domain, heightened awareness is key. We want to identify any movements or postures, especially ones that occur automatically, that encourage your BFRB to start or to continue. For example, without being aware of it, some people will search with their fingertips for possible target hairs or skin irregularities, even while they are engrossed in watching TV or working at a computer. The *motor domain* focuses on the automatic processes that may occur without full awareness of even subtle movements or postures that encourage picking or pulling.

Interestingly, when BFRBs occur there are behaviors linked together like a chain, involved in the picking of skin or pulling of hair. Becoming aware of this chain makes it possible to intervene at different points in the chain. For an everyday example, consider the act of brushing your teeth. There are many individual steps required for tooth brushing, but we do them so automatically that the actual steps go unnoticed: picking up your toothbrush, applying toothpaste, bending toward the sink, actually brushing the teeth (which is often done in a pattern), completing the process, then rinsing the mouth, shutting off the water, wiping the face, and so on. Most people do not focus on each step, they just do them. If your dentist asked you to make a change in your routine, for example, flossing before brushing, focusing on brushing certain teeth, or rinsing with a mouthwash, then awareness of the behavior chain would help inform you about when and how to make those changes to ensure they are made. The same is true with BFRBs. Think about your own unique chain of behaviors surrounding your BFRB.

The *motor domain* also emphasizes your degrees of awareness of your BFRB experience as it is happening or about to happen. How aware are you when you are experiencing an urge to pull or pick, or when you have already begun engaging in those behaviors? Some people are fully aware that they are about to pick or pull, but others may become fully aware of their behavior only further into the process, after it has begun. It is hard to change a behavior if you are not aware that you are doing it. Therefore, in this workbook we will focus on increasing your awareness so the process can be disrupted by using targeted interventions as early as possible. You may have noticed that it is easier *not to start* picking or pulling than it is *to stop once it has started*. You will learn to become highly aware of when you are in situations that are tempting to your BFRB, and to be prepared in advance. Gaining awareness helps give you the advantage when approaching behavior change. Interventions to help increase awareness and to modify habitual aspects of your BFRB will be outlined in Chapter 7.

Place (Environment) Domain

The final domain is the *place domain*, which refers to environmental factors like physical settings, activities, privacy, times of day, and the presence of implements like tweezers or magnifying mirrors that encourage your pulling and picking. Specific places such as the bedroom, bathroom, car, classroom, a work cubicle, or certain activities such as watching TV, taking off make-up, or reading are common "*place*" variables associated with BFRBs. We know that people are more likely to pull or pick when they are alone or later in the day when they are less busy. People report engaging in their BFRB during certain activities such as looking in the mirror, lying in bed, driving, working on the computer, and other common and often sedentary activities. Finally, the use of items that facilitate a BFRB such as tweezers, mirrors, magnifying mirrors, needles, bright lights, or other implements also fall under the umbrella of the *place domain* and should be evaluated. In Chapter 8 we will examine all of these possibilities to help identify the *place* variables that are active in your BFRB, as well as helpful interventions. This information will allow you to make some important and effective changes that make your BFRB less likely to occur in these situations.

Why Is Awareness Important?

Awareness is a critical component of recovery from BFRBs and central to any behavior-change program. Before a behavior can be changed, it greatly helps to understand all of the pertinent details of that behavior, even those that seem less relevant. Sometimes it is the minuscule details that are the key to success with changing a behavior. The SCAMP domains are both internal (come from inside your body) and external (come from the outside environment). The internal domains are sensory, cognitive, affective, and motor and the external domain is the Place domain. Although you may think that you already know all there is to know about your behavior, it is important to be willing to be curious and examine your behavior patterns with careful, non-judgmental scrutiny. Next, you will begin to identify the SCAMP domains that are relevant for you (action item 2.1).

Identify your SCAMP domains

Sensory:

- ☐ I like the feeling of smooth skin and remove scabs/rough spots/callouses to make it smoother.
- ☐ I like the rough feel of the scab and remove it to feel the roughness on my fingers.
- ☐ I like the way the way it feels on my scalp or skin when I pull a hair or pick at the skin.
- ☐ I like to rub the hair along my face or mouth.
- ☐ I like to nibble the hair or scab after I have removed it.
- ☐ I like to smell/taste the excoriate after I pick it out.
- ☐ I like to watch the excoriate come out of my skin.
- ☐ I do not like the look of certain hairs.
- ☐ I do not like the feel of certain hairs.
- ☐ I do not like to see blemishes, black heads, white heads, or other unusual skin issues.
- ☐ I like the way my eyelid sounds when it pops back on my eyeball after pulling.
- ☐ I like for all of my hair to look the same, either in texture or color, or in placement (like a straight hairline).
- ☐ I stroke my hair/skin searching for something irregular to pull or pick.
- ☐ I swallow my hair after pulling it out.
- ☐ My skin/scalp tingles or is itchy and picking skin or pulling hair makes those feelings on my skin/scalp go away.
- ☐ Other: _____

Cognitive:

- ☐ I have thoughts about how my hair or skin should look or be.
- ☐ I believe that pulling or picking helps me to correct something that needs to be corrected.
- ☐ I believe that pulling or picking helps me in other ways, like to focus better or to fall asleep.
- ☐ I believe that pulling or picking helps me to make decisions.
- ☐ I sometimes pull or pick when I am thinking about problems in my life.
- ☐ I believe that certain hairs should be removed because they do not belong on my body.
- ☐ I believe that picking my pimples helps them to heal more quickly, at least I tell myself that.
- ☐ I think that my BFRB helps me to feel like I have accomplished something, especially when I get a good one.
- ☐ I am lost in thought when I am engaging in my BFRB.
- ☐ I believe that my BFRB helps me to feel better.
- ☐ Sometimes my hair or skin just needs to be fixed, I just have to do it.
- ☐ Other: _____

Affective:

- ☐ I engage in my BFRB when I am having strong emotions.
- ☐ My BFRB helps me to feel better, at least for a little while.
- ☐ I feel really good, like I accomplished something after engaging in my BFRB.
- ☐ My BFRB reduces my stress in the moment.
- ☐ I use my BFRB to help me through hard emotional times.
- ☐ Sometimes I pull or pick when I am bored.
- ☐ Sometimes I pull or pick when I am very angry.
- ☐ Sometimes I pull or pick when I am worried.
- ☐ Sometimes I pull or pick when I am scared.
- ☐ Sometimes I pull or pick when I am frustrated.
- ☐ Sometimes I pull or pick just because I want a little comfort.
- ☐ I pull or pick after an overwhelming day to help me cope.
- ☐ I pull or pick in the morning to energize me.

- ☐ Sometimes I pull or pick to help me settle down to sleep.
- ☐ I get really angry/upset with myself after having engaged in my BFRB.
- ☐ Other: _____

Motor:

- ☐ I am usually not aware of my pulling/picking until after it has been going on for a while.
- ☐ I sometimes am not aware of my BFRB until I have done considerable damage.
- ☐ How I sit in a chair or on a couch allows me to pick or pull more easily.
- ☐ My posture allows my BFRB to occur more easily.
- ☐ I lie in bed with my arm propped up so that I can do my BFRB more easily.
- ☐ I usually do not become aware of my BFRB until after I have started pulling or picking.
- ☐ Other: _____

Place:

- ☐ I pull or pick in specific places more often than others (bathroom, office, in bed, in the car, living room)
- ☐ I pull or pick during certain activities more than others.
- ☐ I pull or pick at certain times of day more than others.
- ☐ I pull or pick around certain people more than others.
- ☐ I pull or pick almost exclusively when I am alone.
- ☐ I use implements such as mirrors, bright lights, tweezers, pins, razors, and so on to pull or pick.
- ☐ Other: _____

How did you do? Are there any domains that have more than a few checks? Do any of the domains stand out as primary for you? Sometimes two or three domains seem to be more relevant than the others. This is all great information that will help you ultimately fine-tune your plan for recovery. Fill out the following action item to help you identify, in order, your relevant domains. Also know that over time this list may change. Often the relevant domains may be different when in varying situations where your BFRB occurs (e.g., picking in the bathroom might involve different domains than when picking at work). For this reason, you may need to fill out this form several times to reflect these different scenarios. Remember, this process requires diligence, but it need not be perfect. We can always learn new things about ourselves, and this is no exception. Consider yourself a lifelong student of learning new things about yourself. In this case you are still in the process of learning about your BFRB, and your efforts here will surely pay dividends.

ACTION ITEM 2.2

Finalize your SCAMP domains

Please list your SCAMP domains in the order of relevance to you. Domain 1 should be the most relevant to you and domain 5 should be the least relevant. It is helpful to do this for each high-risk situation that you identify. For example, when in bed at night, trying to fall asleep might have different domains in a different order than when in the car, driving to work, or feeling stressed due to traffic.

High-Risk Situation (example): In bed, trying to go to sleep

Domain 1: place – in bedroom, in bed

Domain 2: sensory – feeling the hair between my fingers and playing with it

Domain 3: motor – lying in bed with my hand unconsciously stroking my hair

Domain 4: affective – feels good and is relaxing

Domain 5: cognitive – can't get to sleep without pulling hair, it helps

High-Risk Situation 1: _____
Domain 1: _____
Domain 2: _____
Domain 3: _____
Domain 4: _____
Domain 5: _____

High-Risk Situation 2: _____
Domain 1: _____
Domain 2: _____
Domain 3: _____
Domain 4: _____
Domain 5: _____

High-Risk Situation 3: _____
Domain 1: _____
Domain 2: _____
Domain 3: _____
Domain 4: _____
Domain 5: _____

Developing Your BFRB Profile

Now that you have begun the process of identifying the SCAMP domains that resonate as important for you, let us start to put together your BFRB profile. To help you gather more information about your BFRB, we are going to ask you to fill out an "Awareness Form" every day for one week to see what you learn. One of the biggest concerns people have about doing this activity is that they 'already know' when, where, and how they pull or pick. We are sure that you know quite a bit about your BFRB, but we want you to know even more. The following Awareness Form will help you to keep track of your BFRB for the next week and it will provide information that will be used to create your BFRB profile. Then we can start to identify the specific interventions that will work best for you (action item 2.3).

ACTION ITEM 2.3

Fill out the Awareness Form each time your BFRB is active during the next week

Please record every BFRB activity for the next week, including how long each pulling or picking episode lasted (five minutes, thirty minutes, four hours, etc.). Be sure to rate your awareness of the episode (1 = little or no awareness, 4 = very aware). Make several copies of the form if you are a "high frequency" person. Some people have hundreds of episodes a week and will definitely need more space to keep track of them all. We know that this can be an exhausting and somewhat tedious process, and we applaud you in advance for doing it! Remember, behavior change is hard, but all worthwhile things in life are hard, are they not? Please pause your reading of the workbook and focus on filling out your Awareness Form for a week before moving forward. Also, go back to the first ten action items that you have completed and review what you have learned. Edit or add to them accordingly as you review.

Date/time	Location/ activity	BFRB behavior (pulling, picking, biting)	Sensory	Cognitive	Affective	Motor behaviors	Place variables	How long?	Awareness 1–4

ACTION ITEM 2.3

ACTION ITEM 2.3

continued

Date/time	Location/activity	BFRB behavior (pulling, picking, biting)	Sensory	Cognitive	Affective	Motor behaviors	Place variables	How long?	Awareness 1–4

Looking for Patterns in Your BFRB

Now that you have completed a week of working on awareness, you will want to look for patterns in your behavior. We find it easiest to understand your unique patterns by first starting with *place*. You may have multiple situations or places where you tend to pull and pick, where are they? Where are you and what are you typically doing when you are engaging in your BFRB? The answers to these questions can help you to begin to gain increased awareness of the different settings in which pulling or picking occurs. After a few days of self-monitoring, what did you notice? Did you identify the specific places in which your BFRB tends to occur? Did you notice that in each specific place your BFRB tends to have distinct, recognizable patterns? Did you notice that even in the same place, there are times when your BFRB occurs and other times that it does not? What is different about the times when your BFRB is prominent? What is different about the times when you are in that situation, and you do not engage in your BFRB? Did you see that one or more of the domains are more relevant depending on the setting and the activity you were engaged in? After you kept records for several days, did you start to become acutely aware of the patterns involved in your BFRB? We hope so! For example, a pattern might emerge that shows that you pull in the morning, on the way to work, when stuck in traffic, but that you can be in the car, with another person, at a different time of day and not even think about pulling. Another pattern might be that you pick in the evening, in the bathroom, after dinner, when feeling overwhelmed from the day. Pay attention to emerging patterns and notice specifically what makes a situation easier or harder to navigate.

There are many things to keep in mind in this phase of your journey. Are you able to see the variations in the patterns that are involved in your BFRB? If so, great! If you do not see these patterns initially, do not be discouraged. Patterns sometimes reveal themselves slowly. Keep monitoring your behavior and continue to be patient and curious. Can you appreciate that your BFRB is not random, that it occurs in a somewhat predictable manner? BFRB activity can be triggered by a sensation, a thought, an emotion, a posture, or environmental factors (place). Learning how and when to predict a possible BFRB episode is vital information and will be useful in creating an effective toolkit for managing these behaviors. Did you notice that your knowledge of your BFRB has increased as you filled out the Awareness

Form? Did that have any impact on your behavior? Did you ever avoid engaging in your BFRB because you did not want to have to record it? If so, then great, your awareness is building and your BFRB is already impacted! We recommend continuing to monitor throughout the entire use of this workbook, which could take weeks, or even months to complete. Each chapter will present a more expanded version of the Awareness Form, asking for you to add more information, such as the use of specific interventions. We recommend going slow and being intentional about your approach to change. Rushing this will not make it go away faster; in fact it will likely cause you to be *less successful* in the process. True and lasting behavior change takes hard work, time, and patience.

Mindfulness as a Strategy for Gaining Awareness

Mindfulness is an idea/practice drawn from Eastern philosophy and has been found to be helpful in many aspects of life. The fundamental premise of mindfulness is that by turning your focus inward you can notice your internal experiences (e.g., thoughts, feelings, sensations, etc.) in that moment (and this is important), without judging them or engaging with them in other ways. With practice, you can begin to be more aware of your internal experiences when you are going about your day. As we mentioned earlier, when you are able to notice your behaviors, you are better prepared to change them. With respect to your BFRB, mindfulness can help you to be more keenly aware of when you are pulling or picking and, possibly more importantly, when you are experiencing a desire to pull or pick. Ultimately recognizing your internal experiences, the urges to pull or pick, gives you the ability to then do something about them. Mindfulness improves awareness and awareness improves your power to change. Mindfulness can help with awareness of other emotions as well. For example, say that I am out on my porch enjoying reading a book when a neighbor's dog begins barking relentlessly. I may think "That's wrong! The neighbor needs to stop his dog from barking!" If I allow my thoughts to anger me further and begin to think of the ways I might intervene in the situation by confronting my neighbor, I have surrendered the opportunity to enjoy the time outside with my book. Let us try a different approach. What if I noticed the barking, took a few deep breaths to settle my body down and returned to my book, noticing the barking but not becoming consumed by it. A mindful approach might be to return the focus to reading my book, while simply noticing the sensations (sound of barking) and feelings (irritation). The goal is to not allow the sound and irritation to lead to further anguish that will likely make the situation worse. Being mindful allows us to make thoughtful decisions and to move with intention toward what we value.

We have found that mindfulness allows people with BFRBs to be more successful at identifying how they are feeling, catching themselves when experiencing an urge, being able to feel urges without acting on them, and to seek an appropriate intervention when urges occur. A more structured approach, mindfulness meditation as it is often called, has been found to have profound impacts on the regulation of emotions, reducing anxiety, and improving mood. We highly recommend that you consider incorporating five to ten minutes of mindfulness meditation into your daily life. How would you do that? Below you will see scripts of several, typical mindfulness exercises. We suggest that you record the script(s) onto your phone and then listen to one each day. You can find many mindfulness exercises on YouTube or on popular apps. Mindfulness is a process that does not produce instant change. It takes time to practice, to build your skills, and to make mindfulness a habit. Be patient, practice every day, and before long, you will notice a sense of calm and of distance between you and your experiences. This gives you the power to choose your responses to those experiences – a highly desirable tool to accompany you on your journey.

Mindfulness Script 1

Sit comfortably in a chair or on the floor and close your eyes ... Begin to focus on your breath, noticing as the air goes into your lungs through your nose and out through your nose ... Feel your belly expanding as you breathe in and contracting as you breathe out ... Just breathing in and out ... nothing to do but simply notice ... Just allow yourself to begin to relax as tension is released from your body with each breath. As you continue to breathe in and out, I want you to direct your attention to your body ... How is your body feeling? Direct your attention to the sensations in your feet. Notice your feet, how do they feel? If there is any tension in your feet, allow that tension to leave, relaxing the muscles of your feet, allowing them to become still, soft, and relaxed ... Now turn your attention to your calves and shins, notice how they feel. Are you holding any tension in your lower legs? Again, allowing any tension in your calves and shins to release, leaving your lower legs soft and relaxed. Next, notice your thighs ... Notice if they are tense or holding on to any stress. Allow the muscles in your thighs to become soft and relaxed. Notice if your thighs are touching the chair or the floor, what does that feel like? Can you allow your breath to soothe and relax your things... Next move to your hips and pelvis. Again, notice how you are feeling in your hips and pelvis ... Are you holding onto any tension or stress? Are you gripping your muscles? If so, just gently notice this and allow your muscles to release and relax ... let go ... Now move your attention to your stomach and the muscles of your stomach. Notice if you are holding these muscles tight ... Can you release them? Can you let go? Allow these muscles to become soft and smooth, giving even more space in your belly for your breath ... Now move your attention to your upper back and shoulders, notice how you are feeling there ... Are your upper back and shoulders tight, holding onto any tension? If so, allow them to relax, to let go ... Allow your breath to soothe these muscles, to relax them. Are your shoulders raised up? If so, allow them to settle down and to become heavy ... Allow the muscles of your upper back to become relaxed ... Now notice the muscles in your arms and hands, how are they feeling? ... Maybe stretch your arms and hands out and then lay them back at your side, allowing them to release any tension they might have been holding, allowing them to become totally relaxed ... Now move your focus to your neck ... really allow your neck to become soft and relaxed ... We hold so much tension in your neck that it might feel extra stiff. Really let go of your neck muscles ... Notice if your head wants to fall forward or backward a little, try to keep it upright, but at the same time relaxing your neck muscles ... Let them become completely relaxed ... Now move your attention to your jaw muscles and your mouth, notice your jaw dropping and your teeth separating, allow your tongue to rest comfortably in your mouth ... Feel your jaw and mouth completely relaxed. Now focus on the rest of the muscles of your face and head ... Allow these muscles to become soft and smooth, letting go of tension... allowing all of the muscles to completely relax... Notice your whole body right now, how does it feel? ... Are you still feeling tension in any areas? ... Can you gently allow those areas to let go so that your entire body is relaxed? ... Notice how nice it feels to be totally relaxed, to let go... Now, begin to move your fingers and toes ... Allow energy to return to your body and become aware of the room that you are in ... and when you are ready you may open your eyes.

This script is a relaxation meditation that allows you to notice different body parts and to systematically encourage them to relax by focusing on each one of them separately. This practice enables you to gain awareness of your body at a given moment. Increasing body awareness is an important part of gaining control of your BFRB and your emotions. This next meditation is designed to help you to become more aware of your thoughts and patterns of thinking.

Mindfulness Script 2

Get comfortable in a seated position on the floor or a chair and close your eyes ... Focus on your breath and notice as it goes in through your nose and out through your nose, allowing your body to relax and let go ... I invite you to notice your thoughts, just check in to see what your mind is thinking about at this very moment ... Whatever it is that you are thinking, just make a mental note of it and return your attention to your breath ... in and out ... in and out ... Our brains tend to wander, much like a puppy dog wanders ... if your brain wanders away from the focus on your breath, notice where it goes ... gently return your focus to your breath ... no need to judge yourself, minds wander naturally. But notice where your mind tends to wander. Continue to do this for several minutes, trying to keep the focus on the breath, knowing that your mind will wander away ... Each time notice where it wandered to and return to the breath ... in and out ... in and out ... Be careful not to be harsh with yourself for the wandering ... just as you would not be cruel to a puppy who wandered around, do not be cruel to yourself ... just gently notice it and return to the breath ... in and out ... in and out ... (continue to do this in silence for three minutes). Wherever you are, gently return your attention to the breath and thank yourself for working so hard to focus on your breath ... Feel the energy returning to your body and allow your fingers and toes to begin to move. When you are ready, open your eyes.

This second exercise is designed to help you to become more aware of your thought patterns as well as to notice when these patterns are present, leading you astray from your present moment experience. A thought pattern might be self-judgment, or future planning, or regret for past behaviors. Becoming aware of your thought patterns in real time will help you to change them to your benefit. Think of your thoughts as the barking dog, they can be distracting and pull you away from what is happening in the present moment. The easiest way to return your attention to the present moment is to focus on the breath which allows you to calm your nervous system and disengage from the "chatter" that clouds the mind. Again, these practices take time and repetition for you to make them your own, so be patient and enjoy them as you practice.

Record both scripts and practice listening to one or both of them daily

We understand that some people resist the idea of meditation and do not want to sit still, even for five minutes. We encourage you to try, just give it two weeks of daily practice and see how it feels. Research shows that even five minutes of meditation a day can have a profound impact on emotional well-being.

Chapter Summary and Roadmap

In addition to reviewing the SCAMP domains of the ComB model, this chapter has been all about awareness – awareness of your unique BFRB domains, your BFRB patterns, and awareness of your body and mind. Increasing awareness of all aspects of your BFRB leads to information that will help you be successful with your BFRB journey. Keep noticing your behavior patterns, even the subtle ones. Just as change takes time, increasing your awareness also takes time. Be gentle with yourself and know that you are preparing yourself to gain control of your BFRB. Remember that no plan is perfect and that certainly no individual is perfect. All we can do is move forward with an open mind and an open heart. We hope that you work through this chapter carefully and patiently as awareness is one of the most important parts of recovery from a BFRB. Take time and review this chapter frequently, practice mindfulness exercises daily, fill out your Awareness Form each day, and make the complete understanding of your BFRB a priority in your life.

Fill out this checklist and complete all items daily to help you stay on track

My BFRB Journey Plan

Each day I will:

- ☐ practice mindful meditation
- ☐ fill out my Awareness Form for every episode
- ☐ continue to watch my patterns of behavior to identify new things about my BFRB

3

Gaining a Better Understanding of Your BFRB

Overview

Why do I do pull my hair or pick my skin? Why can I not stop? How many times have you asked yourself these questions in one way or another? We will begin by helping you identify the "why" of your BFRB. To do this, we must do some detective work and explore these behaviors in more detail. You may think you know all there is to know about your picking or pulling, but we find that there is always more to learn. Identifying and understanding the complex chain of events that led up to and follow the problem behaviors is an important key to effective management. Next, we will identify relevant pre- and post-BFRB experiences that both cue and reward the behavior itself. We call this the ABCs of BFRBs. Before you can successfully navigate your journey, you must understand what is precipitating and fueling the behavior. Later, we will help you to identify and manage the barriers that may inhibit your success, especially those that you are not even aware of.

Before we delve into learning about the "whys" of your BFRB, we want to review what you have learned from your Awareness Form in order to put that information into a cohesive list of your high-risk situations – those situations that put you at risk for a BFRB episode. This is an important step, as it provides you with a preliminary road map to guide you on your journey. These identified situations will instruct you about where you need to focus your attention and also help to identify relevant interventions to be used in each situation (Chapters 4 through 8). Below you will see an example of a High-Risk Situation Form that has already been filled out. Take a moment to review it to better understand how to identify your high-risk situations (action item 3.1).

Review a sample High-Risk Situation Form

Use the information you have gathered through your Awareness Form to identify situations that put you at risk to pull or pick. This is an example of a form that has been completed.

ACTION ITEM 3.1

	Situation 1	**Situation 2**	**Situation 3**	**Situation 4**
Place	In the bathroom, looking in the mirror/bright lights	in bed, watching TV, having tweezers	in the car, on the way to work	at work, eating lunch
Sensations	feeling and looking for pimples or blackheads	looking for ingrown hairs, lights bright	searching my arms with fingers, searching for bumps	smelling other people's food
Thoughts	I have to remove all of the blackheads and pus from my face	I have to remove all ingrown hairs, or they will become infected	thinking about work, things I have to do today	thinking about how much I can't stand my boss
Feelings/emotions	feeling tired from the day	feeling excited about getting them all out	worried about a meeting or other stressful event	feeling tense, disgust about the smell of the food
Motor	sitting on the counter, close to the mirror	very focused on picking and getting out the ingrown hairs	only driving with one hand, not at all aware	elbow on table with hand in my hair, not aware at all

Now, given what you have learned so far from all of your self-study, begin to fill out your High-Risk Situation Form.

Complete your High-Risk Situation Form

Use the information you have gathered through your Awareness Form to identify situations that put you at risk to pull or pick.

	Situation 1	Situation 2	Situation 3	Situation 4
Place				
Sensations				
Thoughts				
Feelings/ emotions				
Motor				

ACTION ITEM 3.2

This form is designed to help you synthesize all of the information that you have discovered so far into one, helpful form (action item 3.2). From there, we will work toward a more detailed plan that includes the specific interventions that will undermine the power of your BFRB. We have provided a sample form first, so that you can see the kind of information that is helpful to record here. Everyone will have a different list of high-risk situations, but we thought it might be helpful to see an example of the kinds of things that another person might include.

What You Need to Know

The ABC Model of Behavior Change

Behaviors often occur in a chain. This means that one thing leads to another, and we may be unaware of these linked behaviors as we engage in different routines throughout our day. BFRBs are actually behavior chains as well. Becoming aware of the chain of events that occurs makes it possible to intervene at different points during the chain. Remember the example in Chapter 2 about tooth brushing and the automatic steps that are involved? We do not consciously think of each step as we proceed to brush our teeth. Once you start the process, the routine, motor memory, and "habit" take over. The same is true with BFRBs. Think about your own unique chain of behaviors surrounding your BFRB. Behavior chains become routine and ultimately form habits that escape our awareness. Understanding the many, discreet steps in your behavior can lead to successful change because it can reveal points of possible intervention to disrupt and divert the habitual chain of behaviors (action item 3.3).

Learn about your BFRB behavior chains

List the steps in your BFRB behavioral chains in order to see the small movements that happen in each place where your BFRB tends to occur (from your High-Risk Situation Form). If you find that your BFRB occurs "all the time" and not in any specific place, fill it out with regard to different activities or other environmental elements.

Example: At work, eating lunch.

Pre-pulling/picking → **During** → **Post-pulling/picking**

Pre-pulling/picking	During	Post-pulling/picking
stroke my hair, search for coarse hairs	find a hair to pull, feels coarse	quickly tug the hair to pull it out
		look at the hair bulb
		drop hair on the ground

(flow: stroke my hair, search for coarse hairs → find a hair to pull, feels coarse → quickly tug the hair to pull it out → look at the hair bulb → drop hair on the ground)

Place 1: _____

Pre-pulling/picking → During → Post-pulling/picking

[ ] → [ ] → [ ] → [ ] → [ ]

Place 2: _____

Pre-pulling/picking → During → Post-pulling/picking

[ ] → [ ] → [ ] → [ ] → [ ]

ACTION ITEM 3.3

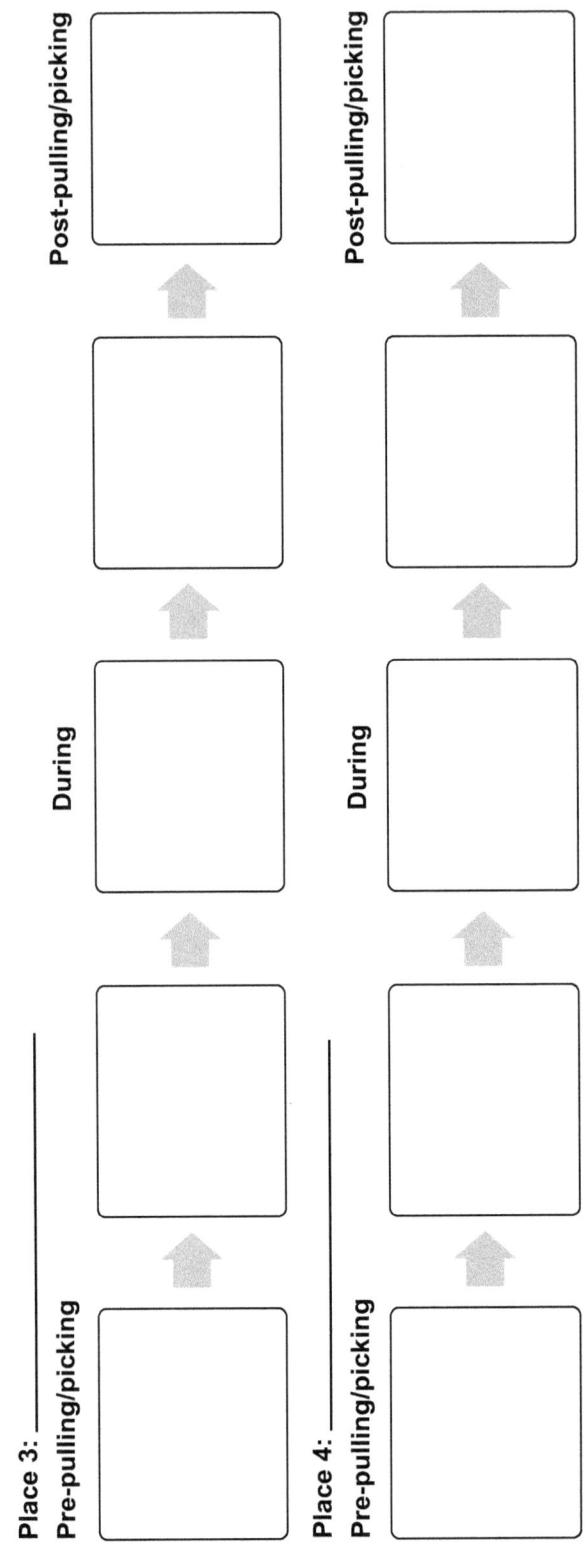

What did you learn? Did you notice that your BFRB is a bit more complicated and involved more steps than you initially thought? Did you know that identifying and stopping the first action in the behavior chain can help you to avert the whole episode? If we use the example provided of "stroking the hair" as the initial action, you might think of ways that you could avoid hair stroking. Remember, you want to intervene as early as possible in your behavior chain. Solutions such as wearing a cap while eating lunch in your office or wearing a finger bandage on your thumb while eating could actually stop you from taking this first step toward initiating your behavioral chain altogether. We want you to begin to think about ways to intervene in the process of your BFRB. Think about things that you could do, early on, to change or prevent the chain from continuing. Take a moment to list them here:

_____
_____
_____
_____

We are now going to look at things that happen just before or after your BFRB to attempt to uncover potential "encouragers." Encouragers are things that make a behavior more likely to happen. At the start of this chapter, we referred to the ABCs of BFRBs. In this model, the *A* stands for antecedents, the *B* stands for behaviors, and the *C* stands for consequences. *A* refers to what happened just *before* the BFRB occurs. Such as when a person detects a rough patch of skin or an out of place eyebrow; *B* focuses on the performance of the *behavior itself*, in other words, what exactly happens during the picking or pulling; and *C* examines what happens *just after* the BFRB occurs, like physical effects such as smoother skin, a more even hairline, or emotional effects such as achieving greater calmness or alertness. These bits of information give us a better understanding of the ways that a BFRB becomes connected to cues that can trigger or encourage it and consequences that can perpetuate it. Exploring the ABCs of your BFRB exposes the chain of behaviors that surround it and thereby facilitates your taking steps to gain control of it.

As you fill out your Awareness Form, notice what was going on just before your BFRB began: Who was there? What time of day was it? What just happened? Also, notice what you were feeling, thinking about, and experiencing at those different time points. All of these factors are important because they allow you to take precautions to reduce your BFRB. So, for example, if you pick your skin when you are watching television, but you never pick when other people are around, you might make a point, whenever possible, of watching television when others are present. Sometimes small changes can be quite powerful. The main idea here is to identify what factors, when present, make the behavior more likely to happen?

Next, we will look at the *B* which is the picking or pulling itself. Notice details about your behavior, such as: Do you pull one hair at a time or several? Do you use any implements to pull or pick such as tweezers, pins, mirrors, or bright lights? Do you pick at certain types of skin irregularities, or do you prefer to pick certain parts of your body, regardless of there being a specific irregularity? Are you attracted to certain types of hair with specific colors or textures? What about the hair or skin makes it more desirable to pull or pick? What are your feelings and thoughts as you pick or pull? Are you even aware that it is happening? Can you anticipate any changes to your routine that may lessen the likelihood that you pick or pull?

Finally, *C* stands for consequences, or what happens after you engage in your BFRB. Do you simply drop the hair on the ground, or do you do something with it? Do you put the hair or bits of skin in your mouth? Do you rub the end of the hair along your face or lips? Do you smell the excoriate? Do you take satisfaction in having "taken care" of something that bothered you prior to picking or pulling? For some people the BFRB is more about the *consequences* than it is about the behavior itself, making this the most rewarding part of the experience. Think about if you were not able to experience the consequences of your BFRB, would you still do it? Some people have reported that if they were not able to put the hair in their mouth after pulling it out, they would not pull it out. The pulling is simply a means to the end. Others realize that if they got nothing out of pimples they squeeze, they would be less prone to squeeze them. Think about any post-BFRB experiences and their impact on emotions, thoughts, or sensations that make your BFRB a more positive experience. Sometimes figuring out this small bit of information can be a game changer (action item 3.4).

Identify some As, Bs, and Cs that are relevant to your BFRB

Review your High-Risk Situation Form where you identified the specific "places" or "situations" where your BFRB is likely to occur. Think about what was happening before, during, and after the BFRB. Do this for each high-risk situation that you identified.

Situation 1: _____
Antecedent(s): _____
Behavior(s): _____
Consequence(s): _____

Situation 2: _____
Antecedent(s): _____
Behavior(s): _____
Consequence(s): _____

Situation 3: _____
Antecedent(s): _____
Behavior(s): _____
Consequence(s): _____

Situation 4: _____
Antecedent(s): _____
Behavior(s): _____
Consequence(s): _____

ACTION ITEM 3.4

Were you able to notice conditions before you pick or pull that set the stage for your BFRB (e.g., perhaps you noticed that you tend to engage in your behavior when you are looking in the mirror and notice something that you think is "wrong"). This is useful information and might lead to some beneficial steps like spending less time in the bathroom, reducing the intensity of the lighting, or covering the mirrors to prevent close scrutiny of the skin or hair.

So why do we want to know all about the ABCs of BFRBs? There are two important reasons why. First, gaining a better understanding of all of the circumstances and chains of behavior that are associated with your BFRB allows you to make very specific changes in the antecedents of your BFRB to reduce the likelihood that you will engage in it. As we stated earlier, knowing the first step in the chain or the antecedents can help you to thwart an episode altogether. Second, we want to know what is rewarding about your BFRB, since people do not typically engage in behaviors that do not serve them in some way. Moreover, we want you to find some healthy alternatives to your BFRB that may reduce your reliance on the existing behavior that damages your body and that harms you in so many other ways.

How BFRBs Are Helpful

Most people do not think of their BFRB as helpful or functional and some even get a little bit upset at the suggestion of it. However, once you examine your behavior more closely, you will undoubtedly discover that there are some aspects of your BFRB that are interesting, pleasing, soothing, or invigorating. If there was nothing good about your behavior, it would be easy to stop. If I taste liver and dislike the taste of it, it is easy to pass on it the next time it is offered. But, if I taste key lime pie and think that it tastes amazing, it may be harder to pass on it in the future. Once identified and evaluated, you may discover that something about your BFRB actually serves you in some manner in the short run, but that ultimately leads to heartaches later on. This can be confusing, but worth understanding. While ultimately your BFRB hurts you in many ways, the truth is, you are also getting some desirable things from your BFRB (action item 3.5). This helps explain the common ambivalence you saw in your Scales of Readiness (action item 1.5) about giving up these entrenched patterns of behavior.

Identify the functions of your BFRB

Answer the following questions to help you identify ways your BFRB may be helping you – even if you are not aware of it.

How would I think about myself differently if I no longer could do my BFRB?

_____
_____
_____
_____

What sensations would I miss if I could not engage in my BFRB?

_____
_____
_____
_____

What do I believe would happen if I could not do my BFRB?

_____
_____
_____
_____

What emotions would I experience if I could not engage in my BFRB?

_____
_____
_____
_____

How would my life be different if I was not engaging in my BFRB?

_____
_____
_____
_____

What did you learn from this exercise? Did you identify some ways that you benefit from your BFRB? It is as important to understand what you *like* about your BFRB as it is to understand what you *do not like*. Although most people intuitively say: "I do not like anything about my BFRB," with closer inspection they are able to identify some things, oftentimes subtle things, that are rewarding about it. For example, some might say "I like the smooth feeling on my skin when the scab is gone," "I like to rub the cool, wet hair bulb along my cheek," or "I like to nibble the hair bulb or bits of skin." These are aspects of your BFRB that have previously flown below your radar. As we have discussed, when you are unaware of details of behavior, circumstances, or mood, you are not well positioned to adequately address them. Human behavior is complex and not easily made sense of. By examining your BFRB "under the microscope," you can more fully understand the functions served by it, and then you can create an effective plan to solve it (action item 3.6).

Learn new ways to get your needs met

List the positives of your BFRB – ways that it helps you or needs that get met. Then, list alternate ways that you could get that need met.

Need that my BFRB serves	Alternative ways to get this need met
Example: to relieve stress	Example: to meditate for 10 minutes

ACTION ITEM 3.6

Great job! Now you should be starting to see a way out of this situation – ways to address your needs without pulling or picking. Next, we are going to look for potential barriers or things that could interfere with your recovery.

Common Internal Obstacles to Success with Managing Your BFRB

You might be wondering why anything might interfere with your recovery. You want this, right? Sometimes even when we desperately want something, it is still hard to stay focused on our goals. By identifying potential obstacles at this early stage, we can create a plan of action that anticipates some bumps in the road and addresses them up front. When you start on a trip, it is helpful to know if there are any roads that are under construction, closed, or likely to be clogged with traffic, any of which would make the journey slower or more complicated. Here we are engaged in a similar process – identifying and avoiding any roadblocks or barriers up front, so we can alter our course to account for them. Barriers or obstacles to recovery tend to be emotional or cognitive, so we will discuss these in depth. Also, we will introduce you to relapse prevention strategies, so you are well prepared for disappointments along the way.

Emotional Obstacles

Earlier in this workbook we acknowledged that shame is an almost universally experienced by-product of BFRBs. Why is this? Well, you know that individuals who struggle with BFRBs often think about them as stemming from a lack of self-control. In addition, like many substance abusers, over-eaters, gamblers, and "shopaholics," they are sometimes wrongly viewed by others as having weaknesses or flaws in their character and thereby are deserving of blame for their behaviors. In other words, there is a human tendency to blame the person for such behaviors, even when the behaviors are beyond their control. Judgment by others as well as self-blame can be damaging factors in efforts to overcome BFRBs and all too often result in feelings of shame.

Shame arises out of this self-blame and feelings of confusion about why anyone would inflict such damage upon themselves. Here we will address some potential emotional obstacles to successful progress in managing your BFRB. Feelings of shame and guilt about BFRBs often lead to a life of secrecy and attempts to camouflage the effects of pulling and picking. In addition, shame can lead a person to avoid social and recreational opportunities and even intimate relationships. It is common to avoid activities like dating, swimming, dining, intimacy, and other experiences because they might expose you to potential scrutiny by others. This avoidance can compound distress by increasing your isolation from potentially rewarding social situations. All of these factors can increase susceptibility to poor self-esteem, anxiety, feelings of isolation, or even depression. The impact of these emotions can be detrimental in a variety of ways that may impede your progress. First, emotional suffering that results from picking or pulling can "add fuel to the fire," causing BFRB symptoms to worsen. If pulling or picking causes you to feel bad about yourself, so that you avoid potentially enjoyable experiences, more pulling or picking usually follows. This can cause more bad feelings and more avoidance. Second, in many cases the BFRB has become a primary coping tool for negative emotions and thus, it is difficult to reduce the BFRB without finding other ways to handle negative feelings. Third, social support can wane when secrecy and isolation become the norm, making it difficult for you to gain the support and encouragement that you desperately need.

One way to reduce feelings of isolation and to garner social support is for you to openly acknowledge your BFRB with carefully chosen confidants. In addition to mustering support, disclosure about one's BFRB can also help reduce stigma and shame and encourage healthier self-acceptance. To be sure, disclosing a BFRB to others can be a frightening prospect for many people as they fear criticism, ridicule, or even rejection – all things they are likely to have tried to avoid. The truth is, there are risks in self-disclosure, so you want to be careful who you disclose to and how you disclose. In our experience, disclosure about BFRBs to trusted others, when handled well, can yield supportive and helpful outcomes that can aid in reducing shame. The goal is to maximize the likelihood that disclosures to others will yield compassionate, supportive, and healing-fostering responses, rather than criticism, judgment, and blame.

If you feel motivated to self-disclose, start by identifying a person, or a few people that you trust and who have demonstrated compassion and caring in the past. Once you have identified the "who," it is time to plan the "how." We find that using a three-step process with the acronym END is helpful. You can remember this by thinking this will serve to END feelings of negativity toward yourself. *E* stands for *educate*. It is useful to educate the person you are disclosing to about BFRBs. You may need to educate yourself first.

Re-read the first chapter of this book or explore information provided on the TLC website (www.bfrb.org) to help you find the right words. A simple statement or two is often all that it takes: "I want to share with you something that I have been working on, I have what is called a body focused repetitive behavior or BFRB, which means that I pull my hair/pick my skin to the point that it causes problems for me." Simple statements that are direct and factual make it easy for the listener to understand. The *N* stands for *normalize*. You want to normalize your BFRB to help the person understand that these are not bizarre or very unusual behaviors, that they are in fact, not uncommon. "BFRBs are behavioral problems much like nail biting or knuckle cracking, lots of people have a BFRB, like 2 to 5 percent of the population, which turns out to be millions and millions of people in the USA alone." Here you are letting this person know that these behaviors are not at all unusual and that you are no more troubled than they are, since everyone has patterns of behavior that they would like to change. You are also relating BFRBs to something that is familiar and that they can likely relate to, such as nail biting, knuckle cracking, or even eating too much junk food, impulsively overspending, or overindulging in screen time. The *D* stands for *describe how they can help you*. A final statement to let them know how they can specifically help you is key. People have great intentions, but often they do not know what to do to help. Without specific information, people offer help that *they* think is useful, such as pointing out to you that you are pulling your hair or suggesting that you stop picking your skin. Provide your 'helpers' with clear-cut instructions about how to be helpful so they can become a true asset to your healing process. Something like: "If you ever see me doing it, just ignore it and know that I am working on it." Or "If you ever see me doing it, please give me a nudge or help to distract me." Or "I would love it if I could call you if I am struggling and you could just be there for me to listen and not judge me." We have found that using the END approach is a great way to let trusted people know about your BFRB while also garnering support. Local support groups, when available, and discussion groups either online or at national or regional BFRB conferences can also be useful for allowing individuals to openly communicate about BFRBs as a step toward involving friends and family members. Communicating with other people who have similar struggles can be quite powerful. Information about these resources may be found at the TLC website (www.bfrb.org).

Cognitive Impediments

We will discuss the cognitive factors that are involved in BFRB experiences for many people in more depth in Chapter 5, but here we will highlight here some common thoughts, beliefs, and assumptions that can undermine the recovery process. Common beliefs or assumptions can center around a misunderstanding of the BFRB itself, which leads to confusion about how recovery works.

1. I just want it to go away.

As with many psychological experiences, anxiety for example, people often have a misguided goal of "making anxiety go away" or "to not feel anxious anymore." While this might sound like a good goal, it is not usually realistic or possible. Since anxiety is a human experience for all of us, the goal in the treatment of anxiety is to help people cope with their feelings and respond to them in ways that avoid adding any additional problems. We are all going to experience feelings of anxiety and we will experience anxiety-provoking thoughts, but it is how we respond to them that is most important. The same is true for BFRBs. The aim is to help you meet your body's needs in different ways which help reduce your reliance on picking or pulling. However, this does not guarantee a "cure" if that means never experiencing unwanted sensations or urges again. It is important that you accept that you are likely to experience these bothersome intrusions from time to time in certain situations even after you have gained consistent control over your BFRB. Instead, consider adopting "effective management" as your goal. By learning better ways to cope with BFRB-related sensations or urges, you can establish healthier behavior patterns, reduce your struggles, and attain greater levels of personal satisfaction. Ultimately, the goal is to meet your body's needs in a different manner, resulting in in a reduction of urges. However, in order for truly effective management, you will also need to improve your responses to these feelings, urges, and impulses so that the BFRB is no longer the "go- to" response. To achieve this goal, it is first necessary to abandon the belief that the BFRB will be "cured" or "go away," and instead adopt the view that: "I can learn to experience these sensations and urges that come up frequently and respond in a more effective way." By following the suggestions in this book, you can learn to accept the uncomfortable feelings, urges, and impulses that are going to arise, and ultimately learn that you can tolerate them without engaging in your BFRB.

2. This should be easy.

Another unhelpful cognition is the idea that this work is easy or that it will happen just by reading this workbook. The truth is that working on a BFRB requires daily effort and energy, but when done consistently, over time, it offers a pathway to success. Good outcomes rely heavily on active participation and engagement in the process. Understanding and accepting this will better prepare you for the journey ahead. Knowing that the journey is not a straight line, and it will have challenges and obstacles to overcome, will help you to prepare yourself mentally, so that you are not caught off guard when you get to the difficult parts. Solid preparation for the challenges ahead is critical if the journey is to be successful.

3. Any mess-up equals failure.

Another common cognitive barrier to progress is perfectionism. We know from clinical observation and from recent research that many people with BFRBs tend to have perfectionistic tendencies. Be careful not to expect perfection in your efforts or to fall into the trap of viewing setbacks as failures. The journey to recovery is filled with potholes and wrong turns. It is helpful to see these as problems to be solved rather than as indications of failure. Know at the onset that this journey will be challenging, and that slips, setbacks, and disappointments will occur. Slips, setbacks, and disappointments are inevitable experiences along the way and, believe it or not, they can actually be useful. How can that be? Setbacks are a normal part of living, and most meaningful endeavors will involve some degree of lapses and setbacks. It is important to learn how to respond when life does not run smoothly. Facing life's challenges head on with confidence, ingenuity, and a problem-solving orientation makes a big difference. Being prepared to effectively manage things when life's difficulties arise is a sign of resilience and strength which, in turn, maximizes chances for effective resolution of problems. Remember, "two steps forward and one step back" is descriptive of many of our experiences in life and this should be the expectation in the case of your BFRB. When you find yourself feeling frustrated or defeated, ask yourself if you are expecting too much too fast. Remind yourself that you are just a human being with the inherent imperfections we all have, who is doing your best in difficult circumstances. Ultimately, your success depends on your willingness to show yourself compassion and to forgive yourself, when necessary, especially when you are not feeling successful and are disappointed with yourself (action item 3.7).

Identify cognitive barriers to recovery

Here are some common beliefs about BFRB recovery. Check any that sound familiar to you in each section. See if you fall into one or more of these categories.

"I just want it to go away." Giving too much power to urges:

- ☐ I want my urges to stop.
- ☐ I am not able to resist my urges.
- ☐ I do not believe that it is possible to have an urge and not engage in my BFRB.
- ☐ It is impossible to change a BFRB, especially for the long term.
- ☐ If only I did not have urges to pull/pick, then I would be okay.
- ☐ My hands have a mind of their own, I cannot control them.
- ☐ Other: _____

"This should be easy":

- ☐ I can stop my BFRB if I just put my mind to it.
- ☐ I do not have to do all of those assignments; I can just do this on my own.
- ☐ Recovery is easy, I just have to decide to stop.
- ☐ If this is too hard, I am not going to do it.
- ☐ I should not have to put too much time into this process, it will not take much effort.
- ☐ Other: _____

Perfectionistic thoughts:

- ☐ I like things to be just right.
- ☐ I cannot tolerate hair/skin that is not the way I want it; I must fix it.
- ☐ I cannot stand it when things are not the way I like them.
- ☐ If I pull/pick, I feel like a failure, especially if I have been doing well.
- ☐ I do not like to do things that I am not good at.
- ☐ I want to always appear to others that I am well and at my best.
- ☐ Other: _____

This forward and backward movement on the road to recovery is central to the concept of relapse prevention. The goal is to keep moving forward and not giving up on the journey when under duress. This next section will clarify the relapse prevention process and will describe how you can employ it.

Relapse Prevention from the Start

First, let us start with some definitions: Relapse is when a behavior is changed for the better, then there is a backsliding and return to baseline (e.g., if you lose fifteen pounds through changes in your diet and exercise, but then gained all fifteen pounds back at the holidays). Relapse is usually accompanied with frustration and negative self-evaluation. Slips, however, are small setbacks that are less devastating (e.g., if you lost fifteen pounds through changes in your diet and exercise, but then gained five pounds during the holidays). Slips are very common, and the goal is to manage the inevitable slips in life. When we refer to relapse, we are referring to a total return to baseline. The goal is to manage slips and, hopefully, to avoid or prevent relapses.

Before slips or relapse can occur, there must be some behavior change that reduces unwanted behavior. As with many behavior patterns that people seek to change (e.g., eating healthier, reducing alcohol, or quitting smoking), it is not like a switch that can be flipped, after which the behavior is gone and permanently replaced by new and better behaviors. As stated earlier, behavior change is a process that usually involves more of a mixed pattern of progress. Although the ultimate stage of ComB treatment is focused on relapse prevention and maintenance of gains, relapse prevention actually begins at the start of the journey. Relapse typically occurs in response to three things:

1. when there is a sudden event that the person was not anticipating that sends them spiraling downward,
2. when there is a small setback, and the person views it as a disaster and gives up trying, and
3. when the person who is on the way to recovery is doing well but prematurely loses focus on the process and experiences a return to old habits and patterns.

These events provide opportunities for the BFRB to return, sometimes with a vengeance, and this may convince the individual that they are back to square one. At the outset, you must prepare for the possibility of all three of these types of events. There will be more about relapse prevention in Chapter 10, but for now keep in mind that the road to recovery is a challenging one and that setbacks are inevitable and must *not* be taken as indications of failure. Using self-compassion, having realistic expectations, and employing problem-solving techniques when lapses occur will help you maximize your chances for success. By doing so, you are laying the groundwork for ultimate success, even in the face of disappointments.

Chapter Summary and Roadmap

In this chapter you have learned about your common, high-risk situations as well as the "whys" of your BFRB by identifying the antecedents, behaviors, and consequences in these specific contexts (ABCs). With this understanding, you have discovered the functions that your BFRB serves in your life, and you have begun to consider some alternate ways to get these needs met. You have also begun the work of identifying some possible emotional or cognitive barriers that may get in the way of your achieving your goals. This is super important as we will want to address them at this early stage.

ACTION ITEM 3.8

Stay on track by completing your BFRB Journey Plan

Each day I will:

- ☐ continue to fill out my Awareness Form
- ☐ continue to edit and add to my High-Risk Situation Form
- ☐ review the functions of my BFRB
- ☐ review ways that I can get these needs met without my BFRB
- ☐ identify and emotional or cognitive barriers to successful recovery, as well as ways to challenge them

Part II

Interventions and Skill Building: Selecting and Using Interventions

4

The Sensory Domain

Overview

This chapter begins the second part of this workbook – Interventions and Skill Building: Selecting and Using Interventions. The next five chapters (Chapters 4 through 8) will describe the five SCAMP domains, as well as provide specific interventions and skills that are useful for each.

This chapter will dig deeply into the first domain, the sensory domain. It is designed to help you identify any relevant sensory experiences that influence your BFRB, as well as describing sensory-based interventions that address these specific aspects of your BFRB. Often, people do not appreciate the relevance of the sensory domain even though it is central to most everyone's BFRB. We encourage you to keep an open mind and consider this information as it relates to you. You may find it truly interesting and realize that it does, in fact, apply to you in ways you may not have previously considered. In fact, the latest research shows that almost all people with a BFRB report some aspect of the sensory domain that impacts their picking or pulling by triggering the BFRB, or by providing relief from disquieting sensory experiences. See how the sensory component contributes to your BFRB, and then you can explore interesting and creative ways to effectively manage those sensory experiences without damaging your body.

Interventions and Skill Building: Selecting and Using Interventions

What You Need to Know

So, what exactly is the sensory domain? Usually, the term "sensory" refers to our senses of sight, touch, hearing, taste, and smell. We will go further and include additional sensations that attract you to particular areas of your body at which pulling or picking occurs, such as itching, soreness, pressure, tingling, and others. In addition, sensory can also refer to internal feelings of discomfort. We know that any person may be more or less responsive to bodily sensations than others. Therefore, responsiveness to particular sensations is on a continuum with some people not impacted much and others highly impacted, as well as some experiencing everything in between. Broadly speaking, some people seem to have preferences for higher intensities of sensory experience, and they therefore seek out stimulating experiences, like wild amusement park rides, scary movies, and spicy foods. Their goal is to achieve *heightened* sensations. On the other side of the continuum are those who are less desirous of higher levels of stimulation and who strive for gentler levels. They may choose experiences that reduce or quiet unwanted stimulating sensations. For these people, the goal is to *reduce* sensations. For example, one might listen to enjoyable music through ear buds on an uncomfortably loud air flight to help reduce the unwanted engine sound and to add a more preferable auditory experience. Or one might put a touch of perfume under their nose before entering a smelly restroom. Sensory sensitive people might have strong preferences for things that feel or look a certain way to meet their needs. Each of us strives to experience our preferred levels of sensory experience, and our preferences change from time to time and in different circumstances.

In the BFRB realm, individuals may enjoy the feeling of coarse or sharp hairs after pulling them out, might like the look of a pimple "popping," or the removal of rough-feeling scabs or out-of-place hairs. Many people are seeking out specific sensations through picking skin or pulling hair, and these sensations can be quite gratifying. For example, some people might like to see the product that is produced when acne is picked (excoriate as it is expelled from the pore) – a visual sensation, or to feel the hair run between their fingers or across their lips – tactile sensations. Others may be reducing unwanted visual and tactile sensory experiences, like removing hairs that look "out of place" or that feel "bumpy." It may feel satisfying to remove a rough scab from the skin to make skin feel smoother. All of the senses can be involved in BFRBs (smelling the hair, scab, or skin that was picked, or hearing the eyelid slap on the eye after an eyelash has been pulled). The following sections will take each sense separately and explain how that sense might be involved in your BFRBs. For each sense, we will give you ways to *reduce the trigger* (*relieve*), as well as ways to *increase positive sensations* (*achieve*). Next, we will break down the individual senses and help you identify sensory alternatives to skin picking or hair pulling that will help address your needs in healthful ways, and that can be incorporated into your life. By doing this, you may reduce some triggers and urges that often lead to the onset of your BFRB and find healthier ways to achieve satisfactory outcomes. Let us begin with the sense of vision or sight.

Visual

Our eyes take in innumerable bits of information each day, sending us essential information about our world. We use our sense of sight constantly for more things than we realize. For example, we look at food before we eat it. If you are eating steak, and it looks like it is bloody, depending on how you like to have your steak prepared, you might decide that it is undercooked or, alternatively, that it is done just right. You might respond differently when petting an unfamiliar dog if it looks sweet and friendly, but not if it is glaring at you and has its large teeth bared. We are constantly scanning our environment for information that will help us to make good decisions and to stay in our comfort zone. Some people are highly sensitive to particular kinds of visual cues and might be bothered by visual clutter or bright lights. People with a keen visual sense might gravitate toward careers in architecture, art, or design. They might be good at noticing slight differences in objects or small imperfections that others might not even notice. Those with a less honed visual sense might not notice a crooked painting or if someone has two different earrings on. These folks might not notice messes around the house or might even dislike an overly organized house. These same people may choose décor that is dramatic and filled with bright colors, "busy," patterns, and lots of interesting objects.

People with BFRBs tend to have a very keen sense of sight with regard to skin or hair. Have you ever noticed that you scan your skin for pores, blemishes, or imperfections; or, that you can see a hair that is out of place that others would ignore? Have you noticed that you look closely in the mirror to scrutinize your skin or hair, to identify things that do not look as you think they should? Think about your BFRB specifically and your sense of sight in general. If you gravitate toward things because of the way they look, chances are you have some visual triggers for your BFRB as well. Common visual triggers for BFRBs include:

- looking for a certain type of hair to pull (color, texture, placement)
- examining hair after it is pulled
- examining the bulb on the end of the hair
- looking for split ends to separate or pull out
- lining the hairs up after pulling them
- looking at the skin that has been cleared of hair
- looking to see if eyebrows are evenly matched
- examining the hairline to see if it is straight
- looking to see if eyelashes are all pointing the same way
- looking to make sure lashes are straight
- wanting to remove hairs that are different from others or that "do not look right"
- examining pores for blackheads or clogs
- looking for blemishes, blackheads, or pimples
- looking to see what comes out of blemishes, blackheads, or pimples
- looking for bumps on the skin
- looking for scabs and rough skin patches
- looking for red spots or discoloration of the skin
- looking for other qualities of skin that are different (scaly, thick, dry, calloused)
- looking at fingernails or toenails for unevenness
- looking for rough or broken cuticles
- looking for anything that seems different on the skin or nails

Interventions That Involve the Visual Sensory Domain

If the visual sense is something you can relate to, it is going to be important to think about how you can reduce visual cues and triggers or *relieve* unwanted sensations, as well as interventions that cater to your visual pleasure and *achieve* positive sensations. This is unique for each person, so you have to think creatively (action item 4.1).

Identify ways that you can successfully relieve or reduce the power of visual cues that trigger your BFRB, and ways to provide more positive visual stimulation

For many people the primary intervention in the sensory domain is to reduce the ability to see things on the body that would cue the BFRB (relieve). Look at this list of ways to relieve visual triggers and check the ones that you think would be helpful for you to try.

- ☐ Dim the lights in the bathroom.
- ☐ Cover the bathroom mirror.
- ☐ Use a different mirror or a different bathroom.
- ☐ Stand away from the mirror (three feet).
- ☐ Get rid of magnifying mirrors.
- ☐ Wear long pants/sleeves to reduce the ability to see certain parts of the body.
- ☐ Put a timer in the bathroom and set it for reasonable times (three minutes to brush teeth, ten minutes to shower, etc.).
- ☐ Wear socks to cover feet and calves.
- ☐ Wear a hat/scarf to cover hair.
- ☐ Wear pajamas that cover more of your body – long pants, long sleeves.
- ☐ Put finger bandages, pimple patches or other blocking devices on scabs, pimples, or other areas that could become a problem.
- ☐ Shave, or otherwise remove facial, leg, armpit, or pubic hair to reduce visual and tactile cues.

Think about at least three things you can do to relieve visual triggers going forward. Now that you are aware of your high-risk environments (refer to your High-Risk Situation Form), make sure that you are using visual interventions in these specific environments. Next, we will want to think about things that are visually stimulating, in a good way. Keeping your nervous system stimulated and satisfied may help reduce your visually triggered urges. Because each person is unique and has a unique nervous system, we cannot tell you what will work for you with precision (action item 4.2).

Read through and think about the following list of visual satisfiers, to see if any of them might make good sense for you to try

The following is a list of things that might be pleasing to your visual sense to help you achieve desirable sensations. Check the ones that you think might be helpful.

- ☐ Watch a funny or interesting video.
- ☐ Paint your room a color that makes you feel calm.
- ☐ Adjust the lighting in your house to be soothing (dimmer or brighter).
- ☐ Remove any clutter in your living space or workspace.
- ☐ Do something artistic (paint, sculpt, draw, cross-stitch).
- ☐ Color in an adult coloring book.
- ☐ Look on the internet for images that are calming to you, then make a Pinterest board or "like" file to revisit over time
- ☐ Find images of gardens or interior design that are soothing to you and then see how you can incorporate aspects of them into your environment
- ☐ Create a space in your home that is your "calm space" and incorporate visual aspects that make you feel calm (colors, lighting, textures, patterns)
- ☐ Play a video game that suits you
- ☐ Find nature photographs that are calming/soothing to you and save them in a file for future use
- ☐ Weed the beds in your garden, removing the weeds that do not belong.

Specific to BFRBs

- ☐ Look at pictures of hair follicles (make certain that this is soothing to you and not a trigger to pull hair).
- ☐ Look a pimple popping videos (make certain that this is soothing to you and not a trigger to pop blemishes).

All activities we will offer you in the sensory domain will include some that are broad, sensory satisfying activities and some that are more specifically matched to your BFRB. Both are important. You will not only want to replace your BFRB with an activity that replaces the sensation that you are seeking (e.g., popping bubble wrap instead of pimples), but also meeting the needs of your nervous system in general ways. If dim lights, velvet textured pillows, and solid colors all serve to calm your nervous system, try to incorporate these into your home/work environment to keep your nervous system calm. If you were to create a personal quiet space in your home, what would you include from a visual perspective? Because there are a host of unpleasant experiences in life which can negatively impact the nervous system, it is helpful to be aware of your nervous system and, when stressed, to employ methods of calming your body down to achieve a comfortable state. Having a "sensory haven" in your home (a place that is uniquely suited to your nervous system preferences) allows you a place to go, filled with sensory pleasures to facilitate a sense of calm, especially in times of stress or dysregulation.

On the other hand, if boredom or low stimulation is a reliable predictor of BFRB activity, then creating a more stimulating visual environment may be a helpful move. Hobbies such as painting, crayon coloring, sculpting, flower arranging, and similar visually stimulating activities might be incorporated into your BFRB program.

Touch

Our sense of touch also helps us to explore our environment and keep us safe. If we touch an object and our skin registers high heat (e.g., a stove), we might take care around that object in the future. We also are able to register pleasure through the sense of touch, whether someone is touching us, or we are touching someone or something else. People with BFRBs report that hair pulling and skin picking are very much driven by the sense of touch.

Many people express the importance of touch early in childhood by having a favorite blanket or stuffed animal that they frequently handled for comfort. Each person's nervous system drives certain preferences, and what is pleasing to one person may be intolerable to someone else. We would like you to explore your own tactile preferences and determine what combination of interventions will be interesting to you. Some common body focused behaviors that involve touch are listed here:

- feeling for a certain texture of hair (thick, coarse, bumpy)
- feeling for short, stubby hairs
- rubbing the hair bulb along the mouth/face after pulling it out
- touching/stroking the hair after pulling it out
- wrapping the hair around the finger
- pulling the hair bulb off with fingers
- feeling for hairs that are "out of place"
- feeling for hairs that "hurt" or produce other uncomfortable sensations
- feeling for a bump
- feeling for a scab or rough area
- feeling for a hangnail or dry skin
- feeling for a fingernail that is rough/jagged
- feeling for anything out of the ordinary on the skin or hair

Interventions That Involve Touch

If the tactile/touch sense is something you can relate to, it is going to be important to think about how you can reduce tactile cues and triggers to *relieve* a sensation, as well as to find interventions that cater to your tactile pleasure by *achieving* positive sensations. We would like you to start by exploring ways to reduce these cues and triggers. These interventions often include reducing or eliminating the tactile sensations (action item 4.3).

ACTION ITEM 4.3

Identify ways that you can successfully reduce tactile triggers for your BFRB and find alternatives to picking or pulling that are stimulating to your sense of touch

For many people the primary intervention involving touch/tactile is to reduce the ability to feel things on the body that would cue the BFRB. Look at this list of ways to relieve tactile triggers and check the ones that you think would be helpful for you to try.

- ☐ Cover pimples with a smooth pimple patch.
- ☐ Put a bandage over wounds that are healing.
- ☐ Wear long sleeves.
- ☐ Wear long pants.
- ☐ Wear tall socks.
- ☐ Wear lip gloss or a lip moisturizer to soften dry lips.
- ☐ Use a nail file to file nails until they are smooth.
- ☐ Put lotion on dry skin.
- ☐ Put cuticle oil on dry cuticles.
- ☐ Wear finger bandages, micropore tape, medical tape, silicone finger protectors, or rubber thimbles on fingers to reduce the ability to feel skin or hair.
- ☐ Make a commitment to not touch your face or hair.
- ☐ Apply lotion on hands to keep them soft.
- ☐ Apply lotion to feet to keep them soft.
- ☐ Wear a disposable facial mask or a mud mask at high-risk times.
- ☐ Get dermatologist to recommend a medical regimen to reduce acne breakouts.
- ☐ Wash hair and use conditioner and a headwrap, leave hair wet while at home.
- ☐ Use a "leave-in" conditioner to soften coarse hairs.

Think about at least three things you can do to reduce touch/tactile triggers going forward. Now that you are aware of your high-risk environments, make sure that you use these tactile relief strategies in these specific environments. Next, we will want to think about things that are touch/tactically stimulating in a good way – things that help you to achieve certain, desirable sensations. This next worksheet will have some suggestions; however, the possibilities are endless. Because each person is unique and has personal preferences and nervous system characteristics that are specific to them, we cannot tell you what will work for you with certainty (action item 4.4).

ACTION ITEM 4.4

Read through and think about the following list of tactile soothers, to see if any of them might make sense for you to try

The following is a list of things that might be pleasing to you from a tactile sense. Check the ones that you think might be helpful.

- ☐ Keep a smooth stone with you and rub it when needing to feel something smooth.
- ☐ Keep a soft fabric swatch with you and rub it when needing to feel something soft.
- ☐ Use a silicone face scrubber to get an interesting sensation.
- ☐ Go to a toy store, hobby store, or search on the Internet for tactile toys to satisfy your sense of touch.
- ☐ Wear soft clothing.
- ☐ Wrap up in a soft blanket.
- ☐ Have soft pillows in your house.
- ☐ Wear satin pajamas.
- ☐ Put satin sheets on your bed.
- ☐ Use chenille, cotton, or manicure gloves while in bed.
- ☐ Wear an acupressure ring and rub it along your finger.
- ☐ Keep interesting fidgets around you at all times.
- ☐ Wear a spinner ring with an interesting texture.
- ☐ Play with slime, putty, or kinetic sand.
- ☐ Use a head tingler/massager to stimulate your scalp.
- ☐ Use tea tree oil or medicated shampoo to reduce itching or provide tingling sensations on the scalp.
- ☐ Get a professional massage.
- ☐ Get a professional facial or use over the counter products to provide sensory sensations to the face.
- ☐ Use a back scratcher.
- ☐ Play with a Rubik's cube, puzzle, or other interesting hand game.
- ☐ Play with marbles, magnets, or interesting sensory items that are soothing to the fingers to satisfy your tactile needs.

Taste/Oral

The next sense we will talk about is that of taste including oral activities involved in BFRBs. Our sense of taste drives so many behaviors and is the source of great pleasure for most people through chewing, kissing, food, and drink. Have you ever noticed that sometimes you eat even when you are not hungry? Sometimes our oral needs are calling out for attention, even when our stomach is actually satisfied. Oral needs can lead to over-eating, smoking, drinking alcohol, chewing gum, or biting on other non-food items. Many people engage in some oral behaviors in the context of their BFRB – biting scabs, nails, or cuticles for example. Another behavior might involve actually eating part of the hair or the entire hair. If that is the case for you, please know that eating hair can be very dangerous and can result in a blockage in the stomach and intestines. Because hair is not digestible, it can get tangled with food in the stomach and can cause a trichobezoar (hairball) that may have to be removed surgically. If you are in the habit of eating your hair, we recommend that you seek a gastrointestinal evaluation with a physician to determine if you have any blockage or other problems that may require medical attention.

While some people with HPD (about 13 percent) swallow whole hairs, a large number perform other oral behaviors with the hair or skin that does not involve swallowing. Here is a list of behaviors that are common and associated with the oral sense.

- biting off the hair bulb
- chewing the hair bulb or hair shaft
- running the hair/hair bulb through the lips or teeth
- running the hair across the lips or mouth
- swallowing the hair bulb
- chewing the hair up into small bits
- swallowing the whole hair
- eating a scab once picked
- chewing on a fingernail piece once removed
- chewing on bits of removed skin
- chewing the nails/fingers to remove skin/fingernail
- swallowing the skin, scab, or nail
- eating the excoriate, nail, skin, or hardened nasal mucous

Interventions That involve Oral/Taste

If the oral/taste sense is something you can relate to, it is going to be important to think about how you can *relieve* oral/taste cues and triggers, as well as interventions that cater to your oral/taste pleasure or *achieve* positive sensations. This is unique for each person, so you have to think creatively (action item 4.5).

Identify ways that you can successfully reduce the oral/taste triggers for your BFRB, as well as increase positive oral/taste sensations

The primary intervention involving oral/taste is to satisfy the oral/taste needs prior to having an urge. It is important to identify when to use these interventions as they will be key to use in your high-risk environments to both relieve unpleasant sensations and to help achieve positive ones.

- ☐ Chew gum.
- ☐ Chew alfalfa sprouts (you can pull them through your teeth and bite off the end).
- ☐ Chew on a toothpick, popsicle stick, coffee stirrer, or straw.
- ☐ Run floss through your teeth or on your lips.
- ☐ Use a dental gum stimulator to provide extra sensory input to your gums.
- ☐ Suck on a flavored piece of candy.
- ☐ Eat crunchy foods such as celery, carrots, or apples.
- ☐ Chew on raw spaghetti, nibble small bit from end as hair-bulb substitute.
- ☐ Drink a flavored drink such as sparkling water with natural flavoring.
- ☐ Suck on a small candy or a breath mint.
- ☐ Drink a smoothie through a straw.
- ☐ Eat shelled nuts (removing the shell provides a sensory experience).
- ☐ Eat poppy seeds, sesame seeds or other small seeds.
- ☐ Eat popsicle with raspberry seeds or other small seeds for sensory experience.
- ☐ Eat sunflower seeds.
- ☐ Eat popcorn.

ACTION ITEM 4.5

Think about at least three things you can do to reduce oral/taste triggers and to increase positive oral/taste sensations going forward. Now that you are aware of your high-risk environments, make sure that you are using these oral/taste strategies in these specific environments. Because each person is unique and has a nervous system specific to them, we cannot tell you what will work for you, but we know that you will find just the right sensory additions.

Smell/Olfactory

Our sense of smell alerts us to danger (e.g., spoiled food) and pleasure (e.g., your favorite meal fresh out of the oven or your new favorite perfume). Smells can have a subtle impact on our emotions in ways of which we can be largely unaware. Although less common, many people report that they frequently smell the removed hair, skin, or excoriate (the substance that comes out from under the skin) late in the BFRB chain. If this is the case for you or if you are just a person with a keen sense of smell, think about ways that you can satisfy your olfactory needs in a healthy fashion (action item 4.6).

Find interventions to help you satisfy your sense of smell, without requiring BFRB activity

If you have a keen sense of smell or are a lover of good scents, take a look at this list of ways to soothe the olfactory system. It is important to identify when to use these interventions as they will be key to use in your high-risk environments to both relieve unpleasant sensations and to help achieve positive ones. Think about how each of these could be incorporated into your high-risk environments to improve your sensory experience.

- ☐ Wear your favorite perfume.
- ☐ Rub scented lotion on your hands.
- ☐ Take a bath with scented oil, bath salts, and so on.
- ☐ Put your favorite essential oil under your nose, especially when entering an unpleasant environment (smelly bathroom, fish market, barn, etc.).
- ☐ Burn a scented candle (when appropriate).
- ☐ Put scented diffusers around your house.
- ☐ Put scented sachets in your clothing drawer.
- ☐ Put a diffuser in your office at work.
- ☐ Buy a room spray that you like and use it in key areas of your house.
- ☐ Put room spray in your car and use it when you enter the car.
- ☐ Put pillow spray on your pillow at night before you get into bed.
- ☐ Put lavender essential oil under your nose before getting in bed.
- ☐ Keep mini-perfume bottles with you in case you need a good scent.

Choose at least three things you can do to satisfy your sense of smell, thus reducing the importance of olfactory triggers and increasing positive olfactory sensations going forward. If this sense is particularly applicable to you, as you become aware of your high-risk environments, make sure to use olfactory interventions in these specific environments, as well as in places where you may need a little soothing. Because each person is unique and has a nervous system specific to them, we cannot tell you what will work for you, but we encourage you to try as many of them as possible.

Sound/Auditory

Although it is uncommon for a person to report that they engage in their BFRB to produce auditory sensations, we do occasionally hear this. Some people pull or pick to hear certain sounds (e.g., the sound of a pimple popping or the sound of the eyelid slapping against the eye when a lash is pulled). If this is the case for you, sound may be a contributing facet of your BFRB experience. More commonly, people with BFRBs report that, in general, sounds can be quite soothing, energizing, or even annoying, as in the case of misophonia (an intense reaction to common sounds such as people chewing or clocks ticking). If you are highly impacted by sound, in either direction, it is worth considering the addition of some of these interventions in your high-risk environments (action item 4.7).

Identify possible interventions that involve the sense of sound

Interventions to Reduce Unpleasant Sound/Auditory Sensations and Increase Positive Sound/Auditory Sensations

If you have a good sense of hearing or are impacted by noises in either a positive or negative way, consider incorporating these interventions into your plan. It is important to identify when to use these interventions as they will be key to use in your high-risk environments to both relieve unpleasant sensations and to help achieve positive ones.

- ☐ Wear noise cancelling headphones/earbuds on planes, in loud places, in restaurants, and so on.
- ☐ Listen to music when getting dressed in the am or at night.
- ☐ Listen to music in the car while driving.
- ☐ Listen to soft music, classical music, or spa music at work.
- ☐ Wear earplugs at night or in loud environments.
- ☐ Wear earplugs around people who chew loudly or make other annoying sounds.
- ☐ Listen to energizing music on the way to work or when feeling tired in the afternoon.
- ☐ Find sounds on the internet that are soothing to you and make them available.
- ☐ Pop bubble wrap to hear the popping sound.
- ☐ Play with a toy that makes a clicking noise.
- ☐ Use a sound machine or sound app on your smartphone to fall asleep or while at work to drown out office noise.
- ☐ Listen to an audio book while driving.
- ☐ Listen to an audio book/podcast while working/studying.

Consider adding pleasant sensory experiences to your life in general, even in situations that do not involve your BFRB. First, it is important that you identify the senses that affect or are involved in your BFRB; then you can add other, generally satisfying experiences as well, such as pleasant music, an appealing aroma from a room diffuser or candle, and/or flavored gum or hard candy. Create unique and satisfying comprehensive sensory experiences and cultivate a "happy nervous system."

Other Sensory Experiences

Other sensory experiences that people forget about involve the interoceptive, proprioceptive, and vestibular senses. These senses are referred to as the "near" senses and include movement, motion, coordination, hunger, thirst, heart rate, balance, coordination, and breathing, to name a few. These senses are relevant to BFRBs in that if you are feeling uncomfortable in any of these senses, it could trigger an urge to pull or pick. We know that for many people, pulling and picking help them to achieve a sense of balance, peace, or internal satisfaction. Think about the various ways that you are soothed internally and then try to add these into your BFRB plan (action item 4.8).

Identify things that you can do to address these "near" senses

Interventions to Increase Soothing of the Near Senses

If you tend to feel "discombobulated" or "uncomfortable," but cannot really identify why, think about adding in some of these interventions and see how they work. It is important to identify when to use these interventions as they will be key to use in your high-risk environments to both relieve unpleasant sensations and to help achieve positive ones.

- ☐ Swing on a swing.
- ☐ Rock in a rocking chair.
- ☐ Go on a walk.
- ☐ Take a hot bath or warm shower.
- ☐ Meditate.
- ☐ Swim in a pool.
- ☐ Do some deep breathing.
- ☐ Stretch or do some yoga poses.
- ☐ Learn tai chi.
- ☐ Have a healthy snack.
- ☐ Ride a bike.
- ☐ Put warm water on your face.
- ☐ Do calisthenics.

Now that you have learned about all of your senses and have identified ways to relieve negative sensations as well as achieve positive sensations, it is time to put it all together (action item 4.9).

Incorporate identified sensory interventions into your Intervention Plan

This chart will help you organize your sensory interventions into your specific high-risk situations. For each of your identified high-risk situations, make a list of interventions from the sensory domain that you would like to try. Also, add general sensory soothers that you can use at other times as well, perhaps when you need a sensory soother or energizer.

ACTION ITEM 4.9

	High-risk situation 1	High-risk situation 2	High-risk situation 3	High-risk situation 4	General soothing activities
Visual					
Touch					
Oral/taste					
Smell					
Sound					
Other (near senses)					

Now that you have a good handle of the types of sensory activities to try, you will want to use your Awareness Form to continue to monitor your BFRB, as well as the interventions you are using in each environment (action item 4.10).

Use this Awareness Form to log your BFRB activity while including interventions from the sensory domain

Please record every BFRB activity for the next week including the sensory interventions that you used.

Date/time	Location/ activity	Behavior (pulling, picking, biting)	Relevant information about the episode*	Sensory interventions	How long?

ACTION ITEM 4.10

ACTION ITEM 4.10

continued

*(sensory, cognitive, affective, and motor variables)

Record your BFRB episodes while using sensory interventions for at least a week if these feel relevant for you. We recommend that you try using at least one sensory intervention in each high-risk situation just to see how it feels. It may not seem important now, but you may be surprised at how much these seemingly little interventions help tremendously to quiet your nervous system and positively impact your BFRB.

Chapter Summary and Roadmap

In this chapter we have reviewed the gamut of senses that can be involved in your BFRB. In addition, we have offered some targeted solutions that can help you relieve the sensations that might trigger a BFRB, while also increasing positive sensory input to help settle your nervous system and foster desirable internal states. The goal is to have a balanced and satisfied nervous system. So often we engage in actions to address imbalances in our nervous system, without even realizing why we are doing them. BFRBs are often attempts to achieve a desirable sensation or ways to relieve undesirable ones. By directly addressing your sensory experiences in healthy ways, your BFRB will weaken because it has become less necessary.

ACTION ITEM 4.11

Work on your BFRB Journey Plan each day

Each day I will:

- ☐ practice using my sensory interventions in my high-risk situations
- ☐ continue to fill out my Awareness Form, including any sensory interventions used
- ☐ continue to spend time working on mindfulness
- ☐ try incorporating some of the sensory interventions in other areas of my life to help me better regulate my sensory nervous system

5

The Cognitive Domain

Overview

This chapter will investigate the Cognitive Domain and how you can tailor your interventions within this domain as they are relevant to you. The Cognitive Domain covers many areas: different types of thoughts or beliefs about your BFRB, thoughts about hair and skin, and thoughts about treatment, as well as the broader categories of perfectionism, and cognitive flexibility.

What You Need to Know

Cognitions (Thoughts) about BFRBs

Through your work on the Awareness Form you will have started to identify any beliefs or cognitions that help to drive your BFRB. As stated in Chapter 2, the cognitive domain involves thoughts or beliefs that typically fall into four categories:

1. Thoughts that are barriers to treatment: Look at action item 3.7 from Chapter 3, *Cognitive Barriers to My Recovery* and revisit those that you listed there.
2. Beliefs about hair or skin that portray pulling or picking as efforts to fix some sort of "problem" that exists.

3. Permission-giving thoughts such as "I will just pull this one hair," or "I deserve this after such a hard day," or "I have done so well lately, I can just pull a few" are examples. These thoughts provide a rationale and therefore grant permission to engage in the behavior.
4. Thoughts that influence BFRBs in ways that are not directly connected with your BFRB, like experiencing worries, making decisions, or ruminating about problems in your broader life: Sometimes people believe that their BFRB "helps" them when deep in thought or problem-solving. Many people report pulling hairs or picking their skin when they are thinking about their problems or when they are trying to make a decision that feels weighty.

It can be helpful to understand and identify the different types of thoughts that you might have about your BFRB and your efforts to overcome it. One type of thought involves expectations about your efforts to manage it. For example, if you have thoughts like: "This will not work for me," you might need to challenge these thoughts with more helpful ones, such as: "This approach is often successful, and I am going to work hard to make it work for me," or "I am in a different place (age, stage of life, different circumstances, a new plan) now and I will be open to the new experience," or "Overcoming my BFRB is a process, and it will take time and effort," or "I may try some of the same interventions that I have tried in the past, but I will use them in combination with other interventions this time."

Make sure that your thoughts about treatment are accurate and not predicting negative outcomes. If you believe that your skin will not heal unless pimples are "popped," it is going to be hard when you have a ripe pimple to not go for it. If you believe that all gray hairs must be found and removed, you are going to have a hard time not pulling out gray hairs when you see them. What we must understand is that many of these thoughts are not helpful and may not true. Alternate thoughts might include: "I can cover the gray with hair color," "My skin will heal if I leave it alone," or "Pimples are part of being human. I can pay positive attention to my skin by using products that will help with healing."

If your thoughts are like those that support further picking or pulling, we suggest that you use facts and sound arguments to challenge the thoughts. For example, if your thought is "I have to pull all of the hairs that are different or do not match" an argument might be: "Variations in color and texture of hairs on my body are natural, and I don't need to do anything about them."

Other kinds of unhelpful thoughts, those that give permission to pull or pick, deserve to be challenged as well. As alternatives to permission-giving thoughts such as: "I deserve to pull, it has been a really hard day," you might challenge it with "I deserve a hot bath and an early bedtime, because it has been such a hard day" or "Pulling my hair will only bring me more stress in the end." Inserting self-compassion can be quite helpful here as well. Think about what you would say to your best friend. Would you say: "You are such a mess, you might as well keep going at it"? Negative self-talk is rampant among people with BFRBs, so learning to speak kindly to oneself is key, but it does take practice. Changing thoughts like these to "I have had a rough day. Put finger bandages on, get into my pajamas, and crawl into bed with a book – I have got this!" encourages positive behavior change.

Try becoming more aware of when you are engaging in deep thought, worry, or trying hard to concentrate, which are all times that people report to be associated with BFRB activity. Substitute helpful thoughts, like words you might offer to a friend, when worries about life's problems are occurring. Other options are to limit your worry (since worrying does not prevent bad things from happening anyway) by focusing on what you can control, not the "what ifs" of life. Another idea is to create a designated "worry time" for yourself. Delay your worry thoughts until an appointed time, for example, fifteen minutes between dinner and the start of evening activities. Remember to prepare yourself prior to the time by using planned BFRB interventions during that time. This way, you are prepared in advance to ensure that worries do not fire up your BFRB. People who struggle with the cognitive domain will need to manage their thoughts and beliefs to change their behavior effectively.

Learn how to identify and change problematic thoughts

How do you think about your BFRB? Do you wish that it would simply disappear? Put a check mark next to these "resistance statements" to see how resistance plays a part in your life regarding your BFRB.

Resistance Thoughts:

- ☐ I hate my BFRB.
- ☐ I wish my BFRB would just disappear.
- ☐ I am mad that I have a BFRB.
- ☐ It is not fair that I have to deal with a BFRB.
- ☐ I hate my BFRB urges.
- ☐ I want someone to take away my urges to pull/pick.
- ☐ My life would be so much better if I did not have a BFRB.
- ☐ People who do not have a BFRB have it easy, it is so unfair.

The following statements are more aligned with acceptance of your BFRB, they are healthy statements about accepting that urges will happen and that your BFRB is simply there. Check the ones that you think might be helpful for you to practice saying, instead of the problematic ones.

Acceptance Thoughts:

- ☐ Everyone struggles with something, I have a BFRB.
- ☐ My BFRB is simply my body telling me that it needs something; it is my job is to figure out what it needs in a healthy way.
- ☐ My BFRB may never completely disappear, but I can learn to manage it well, so it does not bother me.
- ☐ Life may not seem fair, but realistically many people feel that their life is not fair for other reasons.
- ☐ Life is sometimes unfair, and I can accept this.
- ☐ My urges come and go, and I can learn to tolerate them.
- ☐ No one can take away my urges, but I can learn to be compassionate with myself when they are present.

Now, see if you can read the acceptance thoughts out loud. You might even consider reading them into your phone and making a recording of your "coping thoughts" to help you in times of need. Practice each day reading these thoughts aloud and in your head. We want these thoughts to come naturally, to be more automatic than the resistance thoughts.

Perfectionism

Recent studies have shown that people with BFRBs struggle with perfectionistic thoughts and values. There are three specific ways that perfectionism often surfaces among people struggling with BFRBs. One is perfectionism about appearance. Each person's self-image is impacted by many factors, and beliefs about one's appearance is a major contributor. This is so central to BFRBs that many clients go far beyond attempting to correct actual irregularities in hair and skin and will damage hair and skin that is healthy. Addressing perfectionistic beliefs about hair and skin and, thus, accepting that your hair and skin will, at times, be less than perfect is an important part of recovery. Learn more about hair and skin and how to keep it healthy in Chapter 9.

A second area that is impacted by perfectionistic thinking involves beliefs about the therapy process and recovery. Some clients may get disenchanted with therapy because they are falling short of their goals, achieving only partial success in their efforts, or suffering lapses that undermine their commitment to stay on the therapy course. The process of successfully overcoming BFRBs requires you to be able to tolerate the virtually inevitable and disappointing setbacks that will likely occur on your BFRB journey. Your progress will not be perfect and expecting your efforts to be seamless will invite frustration and discouragement. Instead, it can be helpful to think about setbacks as opportunities to learn and grow. Setbacks can be instructive and can teach you about what caught you off guard and contributed to the setback. Setbacks, as frustrating as they may be, are truly opportunities to help you to effectively plan ahead and teach you how to manage similar situations in the future. In the case of setbacks, stay committed and focused on problem-solving and preparation to move forward, rather than getting stuck in the mistake. Seeing setbacks as learning opportunities helps to reframe them in a more positive light. If you think about it, all setbacks are growth opportunities, and have much to teach you if you take advantage of them.

Another area that is impacted by perfectionistic tendencies are those that affect broader functioning, beyond those that are specific to BFRBs. Perfectionism regarding academics, competitive activities, job performance, attractiveness and the like can also negatively impact your ability to successfully navigate this journey. Allowing yourself to be imperfect, to be just who you are, is both healing and transformational. It is so interesting how we believe that we should be perceived as perfect, and only then will we be liked and accepted. Yet, we know that few people really like the person who is perceived as perfect, in fact we kind of root against them. Desiring to be perfect not only sets an impossible standard, but it is also likely to be a social impediment. People seek out and care for others who are real, who can reveal their flaws, and who can laugh at their mistakes and even their failures. We can all try to be more open about our short comings and our flaws, to be more genuine. Perhaps you can even be more open about your BFRB. Do remember, a judgmental person will likely judge you as they judge everyone else. However, an open, accepting person will likely be compassionate and understanding. See how others, especially those whom you can reasonably trust, respond to you when you share your struggles and your challenges. See if they run away or if they stick around, perhaps they will even share some of their struggles and challenges. Allowing yourself to be who you really are is a superpower and can actually make you stronger. Try it and see for yourself.

Cognitive Flexibility (and Why Do I Want It?)

Pain is part of living in the world, and it is universal to all living beings. We do not like it, but it is an inevitable part of life. Suffering is what happens when we judge our pain and try to fight against it. Suffering is often harder to manage than pain itself. What if we could reduce suffering and manage pain more effectively? An approach called mindful self-compassion aims to do just that. There is a great formula suggested by Kristin Neff, PhD (Neff, 2011), the founder of the self-compassion movement that states: suffering = pain × resistance. What does this mean? Resistance is our fighting back against or escape whatever is happening. When we are sad, we might drink alcohol; when we are afraid, we escape or seek reassurance; and, when we have an urge, we do whatever it is that will make that urge go away, even temporarily. What Dr. Neff eloquently pointed out is that if we do not resist, or make resistance = 0, our pain will still be our pain, but that lack of resistance does not allow suffering to add any further discomfort. If I have a blister on my foot while on vacation, and I continually focus on how my vacation is being ruined by the discomfort caused by my blister, that becomes the focus of my experience on vacation. If, on the other hand, I accept that I have a blister and use an appropriate treatment, such as a medicated bandage, I can then turn my attention to the enjoyable activities, the novel attractions, the tasty restaurant food, and the new people I meet. Essentially, I can minimize my attention to the blister and the pain that is causing. Ultimately, I end up having an enjoyable vacation, with some intermittent reminders that I have a blister. And, when looking back on the overall experience, I will be reminded mostly about the joys of my vacation and not about the discomfort of my blister. I will have avoided adding unnecessary suffering.

How does this relate to BFRBs? Often, people get very focused on quickly eliminating various discomforts associated with hair or skin, whether these be urges, noticing something that "needs attention" like a pimple or coarse hair, having to remember to utilize their interventions, or focusing on their unpleasant emotions and sensations. Let us face it, sometimes we just want all of that to disappear. What we have learned through our clinical experience and supporting research is that focusing on these annoyances actually makes them worse. They become the center of our attention and crowd out many of life's positive experiences. This is *resistance*. If we reduce our resistance, our suffering greatly decreases. How is this accomplished? The answer lies in acceptance. Research conducted by Dr. Michael Towhig and his colleagues (2020) have demonstrated that acceptance, a form of cognitive flexibility, is quite helpful when it comes to managing BFRBs.

What is acceptance? Acceptance, in this case, means accepting that urges and other annoyances associated with the skin and hair will come and go. Success involves accepting that sadness, anger, frustration, worry, tension, and similar negative experiences, will arise and reach their peak at different times during the day. What is true, but is often disregarded, is that these negative experiences, once they peak, will decrease on their own. By allowing this to occur, the pattern of trying to force these negative experiences to go away disappears. Getting stuck in a continual struggle against these factors are where individuals with BFRBs tend to end up. All too often, we hear people talking about how to make urges disappear, how to reduce urges, or how to eliminate the desire to pull or pick. What if the answer is not about making urges disappear or otherwise achieving quick satisfaction? What if the solution is to accept urges and other discomforts as part of life, at least at present – something that we can notice and not respond to? Think about having a BFRB as similar to having allergies. A person with allergies cannot make allergies "disappear," but they can accept that they will have to do things differently from other people to reduce their impact. Those people who accept that they will have to make some lifestyle modifications do very well at managing their allergies and live happy and healthy lives. Those who struggle (who get stuck in resistance), may not want to accept their fate and they will rage against the discomforts and inconvenience they experience. They can feel frustrated, cheated, like life has been unfair to them. Unfortunately, this nonacceptance, can lead to unwanted mental and physical health complications, like anxiety and depression. The point is, accepting that you have a BFRB and that you will have to do some things differently can be as simple as that. Those who get stuck in wanting their BFRB to go away or being angry that they have a BFRB, or even getting upset that others do not have to make the lifestyle changes that they do, will significantly increase their suffering.

Sometimes people misunderstand acceptance as tolerance. Tolerating an infant who is screaming while I am on the airplane implies that I am "muscling through" and "waiting for it to stop," which is a very human response, but also very different from accepting the reality that the child is uncomfortable and is expressing it as children will do. If I can achieve acceptance, I can then open myself to compassion for others, in this case the child, and for myself as well. I can reflect a different attitude toward my own pain, as represented in self-statements such as: "So sorry that you have to go through this, but this is happening," or "You will make it through this okay – just breathe." Putting up with, like resistance, is fraught with the idea that the goal is for the "bad thing" to go away. You then are in a battle with the "bad thing" to make it go away, which often is beyond our control, or to suffer while waiting for it to stop. What if you simply decided to be curious about your BFRB? What if you could "lean into" rather than "lean away from" your BFRB experience and try to learn a bit more about what message it is sending you and how you are responding to it? How would that be different? The willingness to have an experience and acknowledge it, and not make any attempts to change it is amazingly powerful.

Cognitive flexibility can work for BFRBs too. It requires that you accept the reality that sometimes you will feel unpleasant urges, sensations, emotions, and other unwanted experiences and you will not run away from them but lean in to learn more. This frees you up to actually make the necessary changes. We believe that the cognitive domain is one of the most underappreciated of the SCAMP domains and it begins with acceptance of everything that goes with the BFRB and the efforts to overcome it. This next worksheet will help you to identify any resistances or "blocks" that may stand in the way of acceptance.

Learn how to improve your cognitive flexibility

Thought Record and Challenge Form

Write down your unhelpful thought or belief, then write your challenge thought, a thought that will directly challenge your unhelpful thought.

Examples:
Unhelpful Thought:

I cannot stand to see brow hair that is out of place, it will drive me crazy!

Challenge Thought:

If I don't get too close to the mirror, I will not see or feel the hairs that are out of place. I can handle hairs that are out of place, and I will absolutely not go crazy as a result. I can do this!

Unhelpful Thought:

If I don't remove all of the blackheads from my face, I will be disgusting, and I won't be able to live like that!

Challenge Thought:

If I dim the light in the bathroom and remove my magnifying mirror, I won't be able to see the blackheads and truthfully neither will anyone else. It is more important to me to heal from my BFRB than it is to have no blackheads.

ACTION ITEM 5.2

Now you try.

Unhelpful Thought:
___
___

Challenge Thought:
___
___

Unhelpful Thought:
___
___

Challenge Thought:
___
___

Unhelpful Thought:
___
___

Challenge Thought:
___
___

Valued Living

In the acceptance and commitment therapy literature (Hayes, 2006) values and valued living are often discussed. We want you to pay some attention to these as well. Ultimately, to live a fulfilling life with a BFRB and to maximize your efforts to effectively manage it, you must be willing to accept that urges are likely to occur and that you can still go on with your life, that is, to still engage in the activities that you value. Think about what you like to do: What activities in your life give you pleasure and what do you value? Imagine doing these things, even while you are having urges to pull or pick. What would this be like? Imagine that you could engage in life, *even when* you are having urges. See yourself engaging in life, doing the things you want to do and at the same time experiencing urges to pull or pick. What would this be like? Are you willing to try to do this? In order to be successful, you must learn to separate out the urge from the action. In acceptance and commitment therapy (ACT) this is called "defusion" where one defuses or uncouples the urge from the BFRB actions. Many people with a BFRB do not realize that the urge and the actions are separate things, not one and the same. Have you ever had an urge and not responded to it? We will focus more on dealing with urges in the next chapter, but we want you to start to think about this now. Begin to notice your urges: What do they feel like? Where in your body do you feel them? How long can you resist your BFRB while having an urge? Play with this idea as it will help you greatly throughout this journey.

ACTION ITEM 5.3

Add new strategies from the cognitive domain into your Intervention Plan

	High-risk situation 1	High-risk situation 2	High-risk situation 3	High-risk situation 4
Inaccurate thought:	Example: I have to get rid of all of my pimples.			
Thought challenge	I can use a little concealer to hide my blemishes, I do not need to pick them.			
Thought challenge	Picking will make my face red and bloody, not a better solution.			
Thought challenge	I can accept imperfection. Everyone is imperfect.			

Now you are ready to incorporate all of these strategies into your daily life. Be sure to continue recording your BFRB urges and episodes in the Awareness Form.

Use this Awareness Form to log your BFRB activity including interventions from the sensory and cognitive domains

Please record every BFRB activity for the next week including the sensory and cognitive interventions that you used.

Date/time	Location/ activity	Behavior (pulling, picking, biting)	Relevant information about the episode*	Sensory interventions	Cognitive interventions	How long?

ACTION ITEM 5.4

ACTION ITEM 5.4

continued

*(sensory, cognitive, affective, and motor variables)

Chapter Summary and Roadmap

In this chapter we have reviewed an array of cognitions that can be very helpful or unhelpful to you on your BFRB journey. First, we reviewed different types of thoughts that encourage BFRB activity, as well as describing ways to challenge them. Next, we discussed perfectionistic thoughts and beliefs and reviewed the importance of embracing your flaws and your vulnerabilities, instead of desperately attempting to hide them. Finally, we talked about cognitive flexibility and learned about the value of accepting urges as they arise, allowing them to diminish on their own.

ACTION ITEM 5.5

Continue to work on your action items daily

My BFRB Journey Plan

Each day I will:

- ☐ continue to fill out my Awareness Form including both sensory and cognitive interventions
- ☐ continue to edit and add to my Intervention Plan
- ☐ continue to practice mindfulness
- ☐ try incorporating some of the sensory and cognitive interventions in my high-risk situations to help me to better regulate my sensory nervous system

6

The Affective Domain

Overview

As you might recall, the affective domain refers to emotions that are present before, during, or after a BFRB occurs. It is common for people to report experiencing notable emotions in association with BFRB activities. People report the experience of tension or some form of discomfort prior to, during, or after engaging in their BFRB, at least some of the time. However, most people also report a variety of other emotions associated with hair pulling or skin picking that are related to the functions they serve. For some, the BFRB serves to decrease negative emotions such as boredom, anxiety, sadness, or frustration, while for others it seems to increase positive emotions like pleasure, gratification, or relaxation, at least while the behavior is occurring. Often, feelings such as guilt, anger, remorse, or frustration follow the BFRB and essentially replace or counter any positive experiences that occurred during BFRB activity.

Affective experiences, emotions, and unpleasant internal states can be useful to motivate us to action and to help direct our energies toward productive solutions. As with other common human experiences however, emotions can interfere with healthy, adaptive responses in some circumstances. Examples of this might be when one runs from a fear-inducing situation when engagement is called for or when one chooses the pleasure of napping instead of getting some much-needed exercise. Hair pulling and skin picking are often a means of achieving desirable outcomes in the short term, but which are likely to have unpleasant long-term consequences for you.

Clinical experience and research have confirmed the roles that affective variables often play in BFRBs. Sometimes BFRBs can provide short-term relief from unwanted feelings, while other times, the BFRB simply provides a positive experience such as satisfaction to the individual. Whether it is negative or positive reinforcement, both serve a reinforcing function and thereby help strengthen and perpetuate these practices over time. Therefore, this chapter will focus on providing you with techniques for managing your BFRB-triggering emotions.

Because feelings are common antecedents and consequences for BFRBs, it is important to learn how to cope with difficult emotions and to find ways to increase positive emotions. If anxiety or stressful feelings are regular antecedents of hair pulling or skin picking, you might consider using mindfulness-based activities such as mindful meditation, diaphragmatic breathing, progressive muscle relaxation, and problem-solving approaches to reduce your stress and anxiety levels. How do you typically manage your stress? Is this an area that you could work on improving? Stress is described as both physical and emotional. To address stress effectively, you must address both of these areas. When feeling stressed, make a point to stop and breathe. Remember the breathing techniques you learned in Chapter 1? Breathing helps to calm the body and allows you to take a moment to then calm your mind. Breathing while using "best friend thoughts" allows you to relax the body and to find words of comfort to soothe your mental and emotional state.

One emotion that seems to be universal among people struggling with a BFRB is shame. The exercises in this workbook are intended to help you to successfully navigate the process of undoing shame that has developed over the months, years, or decades of having a BFRB. Early in this workbook you learned that you are not alone, that you are not at fault, and that your BFRB is simply a way that you have learned to navigate certain experiences, including emotional ones. Even if the trigger for your BFRB is not emotional (anger, frustration, boredom, etc.), feelings of shame, guilt, or self-loathing certainly are within the emotional realm. Not only are you learning to normalize your BFRB, and to accept that it is a part of how you regulate your body, but you also are learning to speak kindly to yourself, especially when you are suffering. Again, consider using your "best friend thoughts" to foster compassion for yourself and allow healing to begin. Self-compassion skills are incredibly powerful tools to help you move toward self-acceptance and healing.

Anxiety, sadness, agitation, boredom, frustration, and anger are commonly reported by people with BFRBs and can serve as antecedents for skin picking and hair pulling episodes. In addition, the act of pulling or picking can be an attempt to reduce one or more of these emotional experiences. Finally, negative (or sometimes positive) emotions often follow a BFRB episode, which can contribute to even more emotional upheaval.

Utilizing specific tools that directly impact emotional antecedents and consequences of skin picking and hair pulling are essential interventions for people who struggle with the affective domain. Interventions such as diaphragmatic breathing, exercise, work breaks, problem solving, engaging in pleasurable activities, relaxation strategies, assertive communication, self-care activities, enlisting social support, helping others, and practicing gratitude can be incorporated as needed. If these do not seem sufficient, additional tools drawn from dialectical behavior therapy (DBT), mindfulness-based approaches, and acceptance and commitment therapy (ACT) techniques are also recommended and described in this chapter. Each of these approaches involves learning skills that train you to be better at accepting your experience, no matter what it is, and better at tolerating it, even if it is unpleasant.

What You Need to Know

One of the hallmark skills taught in programs aimed to help people manage difficult experiences is that of coping with distress. For people with a BFRB, this means being able to experience negative emotions and/or distress, such as pulling and picking urges or uncomfortable emotions such as tension or anxiety, and not resorting to engaging in their BFRB in response. In this chapter, we will review how to experience and learn to cope with difficult sensations or urges, as well as difficult emotions. First, let us talk about dealing with urges.

Some people struggle with urges and find it difficult to refrain from pulling or picking when they occur. As we talked about in the previous chapter, for some people the urge and the BFRB action are fused together, as if they are one thing. Part of successful treatment is uncoupling or "defusing" the urge from the BFRB action, seeing these as two separate things. To do this, you must be willing to have an urge and not respond to it. And, yes, this is possible, and it does get easier! It is important to understand that refraining from or pursuing your BFRB activity in response to an urge is a choice, not a requirement. To help you get better at experiencing urges without responding to them, it can be helpful to describe the urge in nonjudgmental terms while the urge is happening. This exercise will encourage observation of the internal experience without imposing judgments. When we judge our experiences to be awful, terrible, bad, ridiculous, or some other negative word, it affects how we feel about ourselves or the experience. We cannot feel neutral with negative evaluations of ourselves or our experiences. To adopt a neutral, nonjudgmental understanding of urges, we ask you to take a few minutes to explore your urges differently (action item 6.1).

Learn how to take a more nonjudgmental approach to understanding your urges

Describing Urges Like a Journalist

Journalists are trained to report the facts of the news, without giving any opinions or judgments about the events. We want you to "act like a journalist" for this exercise. Take a moment to call an urge into your awareness. It might be helpful to do this with a supportive person present, to keep you from falling prey to your urges. The goal is to observe your urges, not to give in to them. Once you have an urge present, simply write down what you are experiencing below, without any judgments. Notice what your body feels. Where do you feel the urge? In your fingers or on your skin? Do you feel urges as emotions or as sensations in your body? Write your thoughts and experiences here. Remember, be careful not to use any judgmental words such as "bad" or "terrible."

What did you learn from this exercise? Were you able to describe your urges without responding to them? Now, the next step is to try having an urge and "waiting it out" to see how long the urge will last. Most urges only last a few minutes, usually less than five minutes. The time it takes for urges to wane is often much shorter than most people assume it will be. If someone is five minutes late for meeting you at a restaurant, is it intolerable to wait? Usually waiting five minutes or less is considered acceptable. Of course, it is much harder when we are uncomfortable. However, remember that it *still is a short time*. We encourage you to experiment with this (action item 6.2).

Learn to experience an urge without doing anything to change it-Urge Surfing

Ask a supportive person to sit with you while you practice this exercise. Once you have a supportive person with you, try to get an urge going, maybe touch your hair, search for one that might feel good to pull. Feel your skin and try to find an area that would be interesting to pick. Once you have the urge present, put your hands in your lap and start a timer. It is helpful to time urges, to gather objective evidence of how long the urge lasts. It is important to place your hands in your lap or someplace away from the area that you would want to pull/pick. Breathe and remind yourself that this moment will eventually pass. Notice what happens inside your body while feeling the urge and allowing it to be there. Notice if there are thoughts associated with your nonresponse to the urge: Is your brain telling you something about what you are experiencing? Check your watch periodically to see how long before the urge subsides. You will want to continue to watch the urge until it subsides. When the urge is gone or almost gone, write down how long the urge lasted. This exercise is called urge surfing because urges tend to rise and rise, hit a peak, and then, like a wave, they flatten out after cresting. Notice the sequence of your urge: Does it crest and then level out? How long did the whole process take?

How was this for you? The experience of an urge without pulling or picking can be highly instructive and empowering and thereby helps build your ability to resist in the face of future urges. This exercise can be practiced daily with a supportive person, if necessary, until you have mastered the technique to the point that you are able to practice it safely on your own. The purpose of this exercise is to build your tolerance for the distress of having an urge and not acting upon it. The goal is to acknowledge the urge, be able to experience it without avoiding or escaping from it, and over time to not be a victim of your BFRB urges. With practice, you can be the person in charge of your urges, not the other way around.

Identifying Difficult Emotions

Managing difficult emotions is not unlike managing difficult sensations or urges. First, let us see what emotions you commonly experience before a picking or pulling episode begins. In other words, what type of emotions provoke your urges to pick or pull? Engaging in a BFRB in response to a difficult emotion (e.g., frustration, anger, irritability, boredom) is, in part, a habit. For some people it has become the "thing to do" in response to particular emotions. For others there may be actual relief from that emotion with the BFRB activity. Some people believe that their BFRB is the *only way* they can cope with their emotional distress. For these people, their disquieting emotions trigger BFRB activity, and their actions can, in many cases, temporarily help to dull those emotions. Take a moment and consider if this describes aspects of your experience.

What about emotions that may be active *during* the picking or pulling? Do you experience emotions while you are engaging in your BFRB, and what do they feel like? Many people find that, in this stage, distressing feelings such as anxiety are reduced or temporarily eliminated. Some people report a kind of trance-like state in which their distress slips away, and they feel relaxed. Others report feelings of actual pleasure or satisfaction as they achieve some short-term goals, like the removal of rough skin patches or bothersome hairs. Consider your experiences and what role emotions play *during* your BFRB.

Finally, what feelings do you experience *after* your BFRB episodes are completed? Too often this stage includes disappointment, frustration, shame, anger, or some other negative emotion. For some people, however, positive feelings such as relief, excitement, or feelings of accomplishment arise following a BFRB episode, which can help to reinforce and thereby strengthen the picking or pulling. Let us take a look at all of the emotions that you experience surrounding your BFRB (action item 6.3).

Learn how to identify relevant emotions that are involved with your BFRB at different time points

Circle the emotions that are relevant to you at these different time points.

Before I engage in my BFRB I feel	During my BFRB I feel	After my BFRB I feel:
sad	sad	sad
bored	bored	bored
tense	tense	tense
anxious	anxious	anxious
angry	angry	angry
frustrated	frustrated	frustrated
guilty	guilty	guilty
indifferent	indifferent	indifferent
worried	worried	worried
afraid	afraid	afraid
excited	excited	excited
relaxed	relaxed	relaxed
overwhelmed	overwhelmed	overwhelmed
annoyed	annoyed	annoyed
disappointed	disappointed	disappointed
irritated	irritated	irritated

How do your feelings impact your BFRB and how does your BFRB impact your feelings? Some people say that while their BFRB might help them to feel better for a while, those feelings turn negative once the behavior has ended, and they realize the damage they have done to their body, the amount of time that has been spent engaging in the behavior, or the feelings of frustration for having taken a step backwards. It is useful to stop here and make an honest assessment of your feelings as they are impacted by your BFRB. As you reflect on the bigger picture, what are the emotional benefits and costs of your BFRB? Consider the shorter-term and longer-term effects that picking and pulling has on your emotions. Because BFRBs often occur in response to negative emotions, it will be important to learn other, more helpful ways to manage your negative emotions and thereby reduce the need for the BFRB. This next section will provide some suggestions on ways to do just that – to manage your emotions without the requirement that you damage your body in the process.

Emotions Associated with Your BFRB

So far in this chapter we have talked a lot about accepting and learning to experience urges without acting on them. Then, we turned our attention toward identifying emotions associated with picking and pulling. Now we want to turn our attention toward coping with the difficult emotions that you identified. If hair pulling and skin picking are your "go-to" responses for reducing negative emotions or increasing positive emotions, we need to provide some other options for you to explore. Go back and review your identified emotions in the action item 6.3, "Emotions Associated with Your BFRB," what emotions did you experience prior to engaging in your BFRB?

Learn how to identify additional strategies for managing a variety of emotions that are involved with your BFRB-relevant emotions

Identify emotions that you circled in the action item 6.3. Make notes about the suggestions for each emotion that applies to you.

Sad	Watch a funny video, read a book that you enjoy, talk to a supportive person, exercise, be in nature, journal, engage in a pleasurable activity.
Bored	Do something interesting, do things on your to-do list, go on a walk, call a friend.
Tense	Do some deep breathing exercises, use calming "best friend thoughts," challenge your thinking that is causing you to feel tense, exercise.
Anxious	Do some deep breathing exercises, use calming "best friend thoughts," challenge your thinking that is causing you to feel anxious, exercise.
Angry	Do some deep breathing exercises, use calming "best friend thoughts," challenge your thinking that is causing you to feel angry, exercise.
Frustrated	Speak kindly to yourself, remind yourself that this is a process, not a light switch, breathe, review any progress that you have made over time.
Guilty	Speak kindly to yourself, remind yourself that this is a process, not a light switch, breathe, review any progress that you have made over time.
Indifferent	Review your values and remind yourself of what is important to you.
Worried	Challenge your thinking that underlies your fear: What are the chances of the feared outcome actually happening? Use calming "best friend thoughts."
Afraid	Challenge your thinking that underlies your fear: What are the chances of the feared outcome actually happening? Use calming, "best friend thoughts."
Excited	Channel your energy into productive action – do something with your high energy.
Relaxed	Take a nap (if appropriate), have some coffee, go on an energizing walk, do jumping jacks
Overwhelmed	Do some deep breathing exercises, use calming "best friend thoughts," challenge your thinking that is causing you to feel tense, exercise.
Annoyed	Speak kindly to yourself, remind yourself that this is a process, not a light switch, breathe, review any progress that you have made over time.
Disappointed	Speak kindly to yourself, remind yourself that this is a process, not a light switch, breathe, review any progress that you have made over time.
Irritated	Speak kindly to yourself, remind yourself that this is a process, not a light switch, breathe, review any progress that you have made over time.

Think about emotion regulation as prevention as well as intervention. Practicing daily emotion regulation techniques such as exercise, meditation, engaging in pleasurable activities, journaling, and so on, can help you in general by helping maintain a healthier emotional baseline in your life (more of this will be addressed in Chapter 9). Make a concrete plan for committing to daily emotion regulation activities that will help you be better prepared for handling the negative emotions that will inevitably surface in life. What will you do when negative emotions present themselves? Just as you can build an acceptance for urges, you can learn to notice unsettling emotions and not fall into the trap of doing undesirable behaviors (namely your BFRB) to make them go away. Emotions come and go, and with practice you can get good at noticing them and merely experiencing them, without judging them, acting upon them, or otherwise forcing them away. In doing this, the emotions are handled in a way that allows them to become much less distressing and disturbing. Part of what makes emotions so unpleasant is the repeated attempts to make them go away. The initial feeling may be difficult on its own, then add the experience of desperately trying to fight it and you have a recipe for further suffering (remember, suffering = pain × resistance). Attempts to eliminate unpleasant feelings often result in negative self-talk, such as: "This is so stupid! I should not be feeling this" or "I need to just stop feeling this way," and so on. Just like the experience of unpleasant urges to pick or pull, feelings too are part of the human experience. We all experience negative feelings, but can you learn to have *better responses* when having these challenging emotions? Instead of being drawn into the feeling, simply experience the emotion without judgment. Allow it to be there and wait until it passes on its own (like you learned to do with urges). It may help to focus on your breathing or elements of your environment while you wait. You may have noticed that with daily meditation practice you are able to do this more easily and naturally. One of the benefits of daily meditation is the enhanced ability to notice your experience without being engulfed in it. It helps to create space within you so that you are more of an observer of your experience, rather than a victim of it. Have you noticed that with daily meditation you are better able to have experiences and not feel overwhelmed by them? If you have not been doing the daily meditation, do not get down on yourself, but maybe consider adding that into your daily routine in small steps.

Incorporating Acceptance Techniques

Acceptance techniques can also be built into your plan as was mentioned in the previous chapter. This approach involves clarifying your values and assessing the match between those values and the behaviors you exhibit in daily life. Think about what you really value in your life. For example, if you have values that include maintaining good self-esteem and being physically healthy, the discrepancy between those values and those expressed in your daily engagement in picking or pulling highlights the problem. The BFRB diminishes your self-esteem by creating fertile ground for negative self-talk and negative self-evaluation. Having your daily behaviors in concert with your values leads to cognitive and emotional harmony and increased life satisfaction. Working from a values perspective can help you make decisions that are in line with your ultimate values and life goals. Take a minute to think about what is really important to you: What do you value in your life? Are your daily actions a reflection of your intrinsic values? Taking a values approach changes the goal of this work away from reduction in symptoms, toward living a life that is authentic to your values.

Acceptance work also involves acceptance of the BFRB, as was mentioned before in Chapter 5 about the cognitive domain. Problems can arise when the realities of a person's life differ from their expectations of what "should be." A life lesson that is borrowed from the Buddhist tradition is referred to as the "first noble truth" that suffering in life is inevitable, and to expect otherwise is to invite further suffering. In fact, many common psychological problems arise from problematic negative reactions people have to unwanted life experiences. Acceptance of the events of life, even the worst of them, helps us to face them and to respond to them in healthy ways. Acceptance does not mean that we would have chosen that event, just that we accept its occurrence and that we are willing to deal with it as well as we possibly can. How does this apply to BFRBs? Acceptance of the BFRB does not mean "liking the BFRB," it simply means that you accept that you will experience urges to pull and pick at times in your life, and importantly, that you do not need to respond to those urges with pulling or picking; you now have options of how to respond.

Feeling Over- and Under-Stimulated

People often talk about engaging in their BFRB when they need to alter their level of stimulation – to feel more energized or less overwhelmed. Sometimes people will describe feeling under-stimulated as feeling bored, tired, disinterested, or fatigued. On the other hand, when there have been a lot of stimulating experiences throughout the day, over-stimulation can result. Often people will describe this as feeling tense, anxious, stressed, or keyed up. Know that BFRBs, for some people, are a way of establishing homeostasis in the body, of balancing their system. Although there are roots in the sensory nervous system, we put this phenomenon in the affective domain because of how people describe these feelings – as emotions. Sometimes these feelings happen at predictable times such as late at night before bed, after a long day at work, early in the morning when feeling tired, after lunch when having a tired spell, and so on (action item 6.5).

Learn how to identify ways to balance or stabilize yourself in times of over- or under-stimulation

Think about using these interventions when you are feeling either over- or under-stimulated, to help you to achieve a state of homeostasis in your body. Circle the ones that you would like to try.

Feeling over-stimulated	Feeling under-stimulated
Use deep breathing.	Drink a cup of coffee/tea (not too late at night).
Meditate.	Do jumping jacks.
Take a bath.	Have a healthy snack.
Go on a walk.	Chew gum.
Exercise.	Smell some peppermint oil.
Read something pleasant and calming.	Splash cool water on your face.
Listen to calming music.	Go on a walk.

Now it is time to add these tools to your Intervention Plan. Take a minute to consider what you have learned and what you will commit to doing differently over the next week.

ACTION ITEM 6.6

Choose interventions from the affective domain that you are willing to add to your Intervention Plan

List the affective interventions that you think would be helpful in response to different emotions. For example, if emotion 1 is "anger" you might list: "deep breathing," "progressive muscle relaxation," and "go on a walk" as your three interventions. Also, list several daily positive actions that are just simple daily activities that you can do to improve your emotional health. These might be mindful meditation, practicing gratitude, or engaging in pleasurable activities.

	High-risk situation 1	High-risk situation 2	High-risk situation 3	High-risk situation 4
Emotion 1				
Emotion 2				
Emotion 3				

Chapter Summary and Roadmap

In this chapter you have learned about which emotions can trigger your BFRB and you have learned how urges affect your behavior and how to manage them differently, without picking or pulling. You have also explored how your BFRB functions as a response to certain emotional experiences or as an effort to try and solve these emotions, though in an unhealthy manner. You learned how to better manage these emotions through interventions that impact emotions and with acceptance techniques that are geared toward learning how to manage them without trying to change them. Finally, you learned about your nervous system and how sometimes feeling over- or under-stimulated can lead to hair pulling and/or skin picking.

ACTION ITEM 6.7

Use this Awareness Form to log your BFRB activity including interventions from the sensory, cognitive, and affective domains

Please record all BFRB activity for the next week. Also, record the sensory, cognitive, and affective interventions that you used in these situations

Date/time	Location/ activity	Behavior (pulling, picking, biting)	Relevant information about the episode*	Sensory interventions	Cognitive interventions	Affective interventions	How long?

*(sensory, cognitive, affective, and motor variables)

ACTION ITEM 6.7

ACTION ITEM 6.8

Continue to work on your action items daily

My BFRB Journey Plan

Each day I will:

- ☐ continue to fill out my Awareness Form, including the sensory, cognitive, and affective interventions
- ☐ continue to edit and add to my Intervention Plan
- ☐ try incorporating some of the sensory, cognitive, and affective interventions in my high-risk situations to help me to better regulate my emotions as they occur
- ☐ practice mindfulness exercises to help with awareness and acceptance
- ☐ practice emotion regulation techniques

7

The Motor Domain

Overview

The motor domain refers to any muscle movements or body postures that facilitate performance of the BFRB. As we discussed earlier in this workbook, we think of BFRBs and each individual movement associated with them as chains, or sequences of behaviors. We create automatic routines from repetitive practice of movements that help us function throughout the day. Consider the process of tying your shoelaces. Just noticing that your laces are untied triggers a response, one that happens almost unconsciously. The act of tying the laces is so routine and well practiced that it is likely effortless and involves little, if any, thought. The routine or chain of behavior starts without a lot of thought and may be finished without much notice. This often happens with daily routines when, through repetition, they turn into motor habits. Our muscles seem to know what to do next.

This happens with BFRBs too. Sitting in a certain chair, looking in a mirror, sitting in the car, or focusing on a computer screen can each elicit motor movements that have, over time, become an almost automatic routine of picking skin or pulling hair in the presence of these cues. At times, you may not even be aware that the individual actions are occurring. Your hands may travel to your hair or skin, and damage to these might occur without your conscious awareness. So how can you stop behaviors when you are not aware that they are happening?

The motor domain focuses on the degree of conscious awareness and choice that an individual experiences during different episodes of BFRB activity and during different phases within any given episodes. In earlier chapters we discussed utilizing self-monitoring and mindfulness skills to increase awareness of your BFRB. These interventions are very helpful, but we also wanted to offer some additional methods of improving your awareness of your BFRB.

To change a behavior, we must first be aware that the behavior is happening or that it is about to happen. In fact, as we pointed out earlier, it is easier to gain control of a behavior if you take preventative measures before it begins than it is to stop it once it is underway. For example, if, while eating a chocolate bar, I remember that I am trying to cut down on eating sweets, it will not be easy to put the chocolate bar down (because I am already eating it, and it tastes really good). A better approach is to head off the problem behaviors before they start – this takes thought and planning. Back to the example of the chocolate bar, I will probably do better if I do not purchase the chocolate bar in the first place, thereby reducing my access to chocolate. I would have to remember my goal when at the store, staring at the chocolate bars and thinking about buying one, and make the decision to pass on it. In addition, I might also have healthy snacks conveniently available in place of the chocolate bar. Making good decisions in advance helps keep you safe in moments of weakness.

What You Need to Know

So how does this translate to BFRBs? One idea might be to consider using blockers prior to getting into a high-risk situation. Perhaps you would put on a soft cap (to cover the head) or snug yoga leggings (to cover the legs) before laying down to watch television. Another kind of blocker would be to wear finger bandages or gel/fabric finger cots prior to doing homework or putting on cotton gloves or chenille socks before getting into bed. Each of these interventions will bring the behavior into awareness before the BFRB starts and will serve as an impediment to performing the BFRB. Many people will report that their hand will move to a desired spot without their full awareness, but the blocker stops them from automatically engaging in the BFRB, bringing it into awareness and making the action less convenient. At this point, the decision to engage or not to engage becomes a conscious one because the action is no longer automatic and has been called into awareness.

As mentioned earlier, researchers have categorized BFRBs into two distinct styles: focused and automatic. Focused pulling or picking occurs when a person is engaging in the behavior and their attention is on the BFRB. The automatic style occurs when the focus of the attention is elsewhere, and the BFRB occurs outside of the person's conscious awareness. One problem with this dichotomous evaluation is that most people engage in *both styles*, even within the same day or even within the same episode. It is common for individuals to absent-mindedly scan skin or hair with their fingertips or eyes in an automatic style, and then to shift their attention to a more focused awareness of possible target hairs or skin sites later in the BFRB sequence.

Other people report that their BFRB can be either focused or automatic, depending on the situation. For example, a person may pull hair entirely without awareness while deeply consumed with computer work. That same person might pull in a very focused manner when in front of their own bathroom mirror, with full awareness and with intention to achieve a specific outcome. These varying circumstances involve different patterns and would require appropriate interventions to effectively manage the hair pulling. It would not make sense to classify this person as either a "focused" or "automatic" puller, but it would make sense to describe the pulling behavior at work to be more automatic and the behavior in the bathroom in front of the mirror as more focused or goal directed.

For the more automatic profile, BFRB activity usually takes place while individuals are sedentary, and are engaging in other tasks that involve mental focus such as watching TV, reading, or doing homework. Another common "automatic" time for BFRB activity is when emotions are activated, but attention is elsewhere, such as during test taking, when immersed in viewing a suspenseful, competitive game, or when thinking about a worrisome situation. During these times, the hands are relatively free, the preferred BFRB sites are within reach, and the attention is elsewhere – at least initially. Because it is harder to stop or interrupt the BFRB behavioral chain once it has started than it is to take preventive measures before the activity has begun, consider the use of barriers or blockers to prevent you from engaging in the BFRB and to bring your behavior into awareness. Remember, because it is more difficult to control behaviors that are outside of awareness, the use of barriers and other interventions that enhance awareness are useful for heightening awareness *as early as possible* in the BFRB behavioral chain. The key when thinking about changing chains of behavior is to stop *before* the first step in the chain occurs, which is why barriers/blockers are so important for those who struggle with awareness.

There are a host of techniques that fall under the umbrella of blockers. As mentioned, the use of blockers or barriers is designed to enhance awareness and prevent easy access to BFRB sites. These interventions include, but are not limited to, wearing tape, bandages, or gel/fabric fingertips on fingers actively used for picking or pulling, or wearing gloves or artificial nails when in high-risk environments. Barriers can also be used at the pulling or picking sites by wearing hats, long sleeves, long-legged pants, other articles of clothing, or even bandages that impede access to those often-targeted places. Awareness-enhancing tools can be used on either the fingers/hands or on the body part that tends to be targeted.

Other awareness-enhancing tools include smart watches or wrist bands that recognize specific motor movements, such as movement of the hand toward to the face or head and signal the wearer when these actions occur. These can be useful as awareness enhancers, particularly for BFRB activity that is primarily habit-driven and that occurs above mid-body. Other easily available and less costly interventions may also help to boost awareness. For example, wearing noisy bangle bracelets can enhance awareness, as can finger bandages and other blocking devices.

Habit reversal therapy or HRT is an intervention developed by Azrin and his colleagues in the 1970s that focuses on self-monitoring, as well as the use of "competing motor responses" (actions) to interfere with the ability to pull or pick. These are valid and potentially useful interventions that are incorporated into ComB techniques. For example, fist clenching involves clenching your fists and holding the clench for at least a minute or until the urge passes, after you pull a hair or if you are experiencing an urge to do so. The idea is that you perform another activity, one that makes it hard to pull or pick, and that new activity then becomes the "go-to" activity in the trigger situation. Another intervention included in HRT is to have the individual change their physical posture to make pulling or picking less convenient. For example, if you tend to pull while sitting with your elbow resting on the arm of your couch, you might try sitting in the middle of the couch or on an armless chair with your hands folded at your side.

Since the beginning of ComB treatment, we have recommended expansion of competitive responses to include activities such as manipulating objects like putty or clay, playing with varieties of "hand toys," engaging in self-care activities like polishing one's nails, massaging the scalp, or applying healing/beauty products to their hair or skin in high-risk situations. With all of these types of interventions, the goals are to increase awareness of the BFRB and to encourage engagement in an activity that "competes" with the performance of the BFRB. Competing responses are best utilized in more motor-driven situations where you are not fully aware that your BFRB chain of actions has already begun and your BFRB is more automatic in nature. Think about what these situations are in your life. Where and when do you start to pull or pick without full awareness?

This discussion would not be complete if we did not mention the "trance-like state" that many people report while engaging in their BFRB. It is common for people to report that while they are pulling or picking, they are completely zoned out and in a sort of trance, unaware of things going on around them, oblivious to time, and feeling out of control of their behavior. Clinical experience tells us that these times can be tracked and often occur in predictable patterns as well. Knowing the sequence of actions and specific situations where these states occur can help you prepare and, hopefully, avoid them going forward. For example, if you have observed that these times of hyper-focus happen most often when you are alone, in bed, late at night, with the light turned on, after having had a hard day, this would be an excellent time to prepare yourself to prevent the trance from happening by using the blockers discussed here. In this case, one might try going to bed a little later and immediately turn off the light. At the same time, one might wear gloves and a soft beanie to prevent any habitual behavior from starting (action item 7.1).

Learn an array of interventions to help in the motor domain

Check the motor domain interventions that you think might be helpful to try. Remember, these are interventions for you to use to both increase your awareness and decrease your ability to pull or pick.

Blockers:

- ☐ Wear a hat in high-risk areas.
- ☐ Wear gloves/mittens in high-risk areas.
- ☐ Wear band aids over fingertips.
- ☐ Wear rubber fingertips/silicone finger protectors/rubber thimbles (used for clerical workers).
- ☐ Wear long sleeved shirts, long pants, or socks.
- ☐ Wear a hat, scarf, or bandana.
- ☐ Wear glasses to prevent touching lashes/brows.
- ☐ Put Vaseline on the lashes/brows.
- ☐ Wear a wide head band.
- ☐ Wear an elbow brace (to make it hard to bend the elbow without awareness).
- ☐ Wear a thumb brace.
- ☐ Wear a sleep mask to cover eyelashes and eyebrows.
- ☐ Wear a gel mask to cover eyebrows and provide some sensory input to the site.
- ☐ Wear a bungee fastened to the belt and wrist to inhibit hands from moving toward a picking or pulling site.

Postural Changes:

- ☐ Change where you sit when participating in a certain high-risk activity.
- ☐ Change your posture while sitting (e.g., do not prop your elbow up on the armrest so that your hand can stroke your hair).
- ☐ Sit upright in bed.
- ☐ Do not lean over the countertop to look in the mirror.
- ☐ Sit on your hands.
- ☐ Clench your fists.

Environmental Changes That Increase Awareness:

- ☐ Put a bandage on scabs, wounds, or rough patches.
- ☐ Cut fingernails short.
- ☐ Put pungent stuff (like perfume or aftershave) on fingers to raise awareness and help keep fingers away from BFRB sites.
- ☐ Cut hair or wear hair in a ponytail.
- ☐ Wash hair.
- ☐ Wear long sleeves, long pants, or socks.
- ☐ Put lotion on the skin.
- ☐ Change posture.
- ☐ Get fake nails put on fingers to help reduce the ability to pull hair.

Now think about your high-risk situations: What motor interventions might you try in each high-risk situation? Think about what is socially appropriate in various contexts, what is easy for you to manage, and what is doable in your lifestyle (action item 7.2).

Identify specific interventions to use in your high-risk situations on your Intervention Plan

List the motoric interventions that you think would be helpful in your different high-risk situations.

ACTION ITEM 7.2

	High-risk situation 1	High-risk situation 2	High-risk situation 3	High-risk situation 4
Blocker 1				
Blocker 2				
Blocker 3				
Blocker 4				
Environmental change				
Postural change				

Interventions and Skill Building: Selecting and Using Interventions

Chapter Summary and Roadmap

In this chapter you have identified specific aspects of your BFRB that might be occurring outside of your conscious awareness. A main point of this chapter is to help you to become even more aware of the chain of events that occurs with each episode of your BFRB. You learned about a host of techniques that can help to increase your awareness when you are in specific situations, those situations where you are not keenly aware of your BFRB as it is happening. In addition to using blocks or barriers, you will want to continue to work on your weekly goals on your weekly plan.

Use this Awareness From to record all BFRB urges/episodes including all of the interventions that you used

Please record every BFRB activity for the next week. Also, record the sensory, cognitive, affective, and motor interventions that you used.

Date/time	Location/ activity	Behavior (pulling, picking, biting)	Relevant information about the episode*	Sensory interventions	Cognitive interventions	Affective interventions	Motoric interventions	How long?

ACTION ITEM 7.3

continued

ACTION ITEM 7.3

*(sensory, cognitive, affective, and motor variables)

Remember to make sure that you have available the items that you need to help you in your high-risk situations (gloves, finger bandages, rubber fingers, etc.) and have them available across different BFRB environments.

Continue to work on your action items daily

Each day I will:

- ☐ continue to fill out my Awareness Form
- ☐ continue to edit and add to my Intervention Plan
- ☐ try incorporating some of the sensory, cognitive, affective, and motor interventions in my high-risk situations to help me to better prevent my BFRB from occurring and to enhance my awareness

8

The Place Domain

Overview

This chapter will help you identify relevant environments, activities, times of day, or other details about external factors in your life that may facilitate the occurrence of your BFRB. We will also focus on interventions that could be most helpful given the specific place triggers that you have identified through your Awareness Form. Please understand that BFRBs do not always occur for people only in specific places or during specific activities. There will be some readers who do not relate to this at all; they might be thinking: "My BFRB is more related to emotions or sensations than to certain places … it can happen anywhere." If this is true for you, please be patient, we will get there. We cover place/activity because most people with a BFRB do report at least some environmental cues that trigger their episodes. Although the word "place" implies a simple location, the place domain of the SCAMP model refers to much more than that. Place refers to the following external, situational variables, each of which will be covered in greater detail in this chapter:

- physical location
- time of day
- lighting
- presence or absence of other people
- implements
- activities

What You Need to Know

Physical Location

Certain physical locations tend to be common settings for BFRB activity. Often these locations include the bedroom, bathroom, study, classroom, office, family room, at a desk, or in a car. In each of these settings the person is sitting or lying down with at least one hand free. Remember our discussion about motor movements and muscle memory? In such places, you are comfortably positioned to have easy access to a picking or pulling site. Think about when you are working on your computer in deep concentration. Does your hand travel to your skin, your fingernails, your scalp, or other area where hair can be touched? This is the motor habit taking over. A focus on the place domain gives you an opportunity to change things a bit and make the environment less convenient or less appealing to pick skin or pull hair. Sometimes moving to a "high traffic" space such as the kitchen, dining room, common lounge area, or to the main reading room of a library instead of more private locations helps inhibit BFRB activity. Changing the room and the experience within it can be a helpful part of managing your BFRB.

Another place where people commonly experience problems is the bathroom. Not only is it well lit, but it usually assures privacy, has a large mirror and bright lights, and may contain tweezers or other implements such as a magnifying mirror that are used to facilitate pulling or picking. Again, keep in mind that change in the bathroom environment can provide opportunities for helping manage your BFRB. Lowering the intensity of the bathroom lighting or covering the mirror may reduce the likelihood that you will scrutinize spots on your skin, eyelashes, eyebrows, or other potential BFRB sites. Often people will ask how they can manage brushing their teeth, applying their makeup, or brushing their hair without a mirror. When it is feasible, we suggest that you try covering half of the mirror (top or bottom) with wrapping paper. In this way, when you cleanse or groom yourself, such as when brushing your teeth, shaving, or putting on makeup, you will have to bend down or stand stretching extra tall. Either way, it is less comfortable and makes it a bit harder to get stuck picking or pulling. Making changes, large or small, in the rooms where your BFRB typically occurs is an important part of the management plan.

Time of Day

Often people will report that their BFRB is particularly tough to manage at certain times of the day. For some, coming home from work can be a very challenging time. All you may want to do is sit, relax, and decompress. Unfortunately, this may include routine bouts of picking or pulling. If this is the case, you may want to do something different as soon as you get home, like sitting with a cup of newly brewed tea, meditating, or taking a quick shower. Activities like these can be relaxing and give you an opportunity to decompress without picking or pulling. If these do not appeal to you, consider going for a walk, a jog, or engaging in other kinds of mild exercise. Changing your routine so that you do not fall prey to problem behaviors during predictable times of the day can be extremely helpful in managing your BFRB.

Lighting

Often well-lit places are a trigger for picking or pulling because they allow you to see things that you might otherwise overlook. Using a brightly lit magnifying mirror can provide powerful visual triggers and having one available is dangerous. Magnifying mirrors should be removed completely if you use one. Adding a dimmer to the light switch is a relatively inexpensive way to reduce the risk of visual triggers. If this is not an option, you can tape the light switch down and put a less bright lamp in that room for lower illumination. A lamp will provide enough light to see well enough for most tasks, but not so much light that highlight details of skin or hair that might trigger a BFRB episode.

Implements

When implements are involved, removing them is often an effective strategy, but it may not always make sense to do so. For example, if it seems essential to have tweezers available for occasional use, they can be placed in a sealable plastic bag filled with water and kept in the freezer. This way, when there is a legitimate need for the tweezers, you can still use them, defrosting them in hot water when needed. This may seem extreme to some people but be assured that interventions such as this are temporary. Sometimes we have to make more extreme changes in early stages of BFRB management to ensure success over the longer term. The goal is to make the use of implements less impulsive and more thoughtfully considered. Alternative problem-solving approaches should be explored creatively. As further examples, you could place tweezers, needles, pimple-picking implements, or other tools in a less convenient spot such as at the far end of your house or apartment or even in the trunk of your car. Requiring a greater effort to fetch the item encourages thought and planning rather than immediate reactivity. We will emphasize again that magnifying mirrors can be dangerous for people with BFRBs and should be removed altogether in almost all cases. Seeing details of one's face or hair at that magnification rarely results in feelings of pleasure or satisfaction. Most often, visual triggers will result in movement along the BFRB chain of behaviors. Therefore, we recommend getting rid of them, at least for the time that you are actively working on managing your BFRB.

Presence or Absence of Other People

If you are like most people with a BFRB, you are more likely to engage in your BFRB when you are alone than when you are with other people. Sometimes whether or not the BFRB is performed is dependent on the presence or absence of certain people. For example, a person might pull hair at school, in front of classmates, but not in front of her parents, or vice versa. Knowing your unique BFRB habits and styles will help to guide you in your BFRB intervention plan. Look over your Awareness Forms and see if you can identify patterns that include the presence or absence of other people. While it is impossible and therefore not advisable to plan to "never be alone," there are times when being alone is a definite problem. For example, if pulling or picking usually takes place after work, in the bedroom, while others are in other areas of the house, you might consider avoiding the bedroom and staying in the presence of others during that time. Planning to go for a walk, cook dinner with a family member, or watch TV with others can ensure that this high-risk time is circumvented. Keeping your door open at work to reduce the privacy and solitude of being alone in the office can be a useful change. Some environments such as using the bathroom require more privacy, therefore preparing the space so that you might be safely alone for a short time will help. Setting a timer, using blockers, and dimming the lights are all helpful when in a high-risk environment alone. Be creative and make a point to reduce risk in situations where your BFRB is exacerbated by being alone.

Activity

Some people find that while involved in certain activities, they may repeatedly get stuck in a cycle of hair pulling or skin picking. These activities include watching TV, working on the computer, reading, lying in bed, or in the bathroom. Do any of these apply to you? Many people who struggle with BFRBs may be aware that they have more trouble in circumstances like these, but do not know how to go about changing these patterns. One idea that often comes up is to just avoid these situations – "I just will not watch TV!". We do not think this a reasonable long-term solution in most cases, but it can be a short-term approach that can allow for reduction of symptoms, especially in the early stages of your journey. Early success with more restrictive measures can lead to increased confidence and a sense of control and mastery as secondary benefits. Many people are not willing to give up TV watching, even temporarily. This is not unreasonable; however, we suggest that you plan ahead when entering the room where you will watch TV. You might try sitting in a different location (a spot that requires you sit up with hands positioned away from your hair and skin rather than lounging with your hand near customary BFRB sites). Have fidget toys or other items for manipulation placed near where you sit and use them before turning on the TV. Wear a hat, use other blockers, or watch TV when others are present to change the likelihood that you will engage in your BFRB. Whatever you decide, choose things that will make you both aware of what your hands are doing and that make picking and pulling less likely to occur (action item 8.1).

Identify relevant place variables so that you can begin to develop your Intervention Plan – refer back to your Awareness Form to identify all of the relevant place variables that impact the performance of your BFRB

Review the following place variables to see which ones refer to you and your BFRB.

Many of these you will already have identified on your Awareness Form.

ACTION ITEM 8.1

Physical Location:

- ☐ bedroom
- ☐ bathroom
- ☐ dorm room
- ☐ car
- ☐ kitchen
- ☐ family room
- ☐ office
- ☐ nursery
- ☐ classroom
- ☐ library
- ☐ elevator
- ☐ movie theater
- ☐ other: _____

Activity:

- ☐ trying to fall asleep
- ☐ reading a book
- ☐ playing a game
- ☐ resting
- ☐ playing on the phone
- ☐ watching TV
- ☐ awake in the middle of the night
- ☐ going to the bathroom
- ☐ getting ready to shower
- ☐ just finished showering/bathing
- ☐ brushing my teeth
- ☐ putting on makeup
- ☐ washing my face
- ☐ looking in the mirror
- ☐ driving
- ☐ stuck in traffic
- ☐ cooking
- ☐ working
- ☐ concentrating
- ☐ searching the web
- ☐ in a meeting
- ☐ feeding the baby
- ☐ listening to a lecture
- ☐ taking a test
- ☐ writing a paper/document
- ☐ studying
- ☐ watching a movie
- ☐ other: _____

Time of Day:

- ☐ morning
- ☐ afternoon
- ☐ evening
- ☐ late night

Lighting:

- ☐ bright lights
- ☐ mirror with lights
- ☐ total darkness

Presence or Absence of Other People:

- ☐ No one is around, I am alone.
- ☐ People are around, but no one is looking.
- ☐ People are around, but I am sneaky.
- ☐ People are around, and I do not care.

Implements:

- ☐ tweezers
- ☐ mirrors/magnifying mirrors
- ☐ pins/needles
- ☐ acne picking tools
- ☐ other: _____

Interventions for the Place Domain

If place is an important feature of your BFRB, let us identify some interventions that might be useful for you in that domain. Sometimes it is easy to simply leave a location, take a break from an activity, or avoid the circumstance altogether. If I am trying to eat healthfully, I can avoid going to the bakery or the candy store without much of a problem. However, if you are likely to pull in the bathroom, there are not really other good options. In cases where a place cannot be avoided (e.g., school, work, car, bed, or bathroom), you will want to thoughtfully modify them to help you to be successful (action item 8.2).

ACTION ITEM 8.2

Identify interventions for various place variables to help you to better manage your BFRB

Here is a list of interventions that can help with the place domain. Remember, if a place can be avoided, it is best to. Otherwise, limit the time spent in this environment or to try to be in that environment at times when the BFRB is less likely to happen. Check the interventions that you would be willing to try.

- ☐ Wear "blockers" when falling asleep (cap, gloves, finger bandages, long sleeves, long pants, etc.).
- ☐ Limit the time spent in the bathroom (use a timer to alert you that your time is up).
- ☐ Leave the bathroom while the shower heats up, and shower immediately upon reentering.
- ☐ Leave the bathroom as soon as you are finished showering.
- ☐ Have many toys/fidgets within reach of the toilet.
- ☐ Watch TV when others are present.
- ☐ Watch TV at times when you are unlikely to pull/pick.
- ☐ Limit TV watching.
- ☐ Wear blockers when watching TV.
- ☐ Read in a common area where others are present.
- ☐ Read at a time when you are less likely to pull/pick.
- ☐ Wear blocks when you are reading.
- ☐ Dim the lights in the bathroom.
- ☐ Stand three feet from the mirror in the bathroom.
- ☐ Cover the mirror.
- ☐ Move BFRB implements (tweezers, needles, pins, sharp objects, tools, etc.) out of the bathroom and to a place that is inconvenient (like the trunk of your car or in the attic).
- ☐ Get rid of magnifying mirrors.
- ☐ Get up and leave an environment where you are feeling an urge.
- ☐ Take frequent breaks from activities that you associate with your BFRB (e.g., reading, watching tv, playing on phone).

Now it is time to incorporate these ideas into your Intervention Plan. Take a minute to add what you have learned and what you will commit to making changes over the next week (action item 8.3).

Identify specific interventions to use in your high-risk situations on your Intervention Plan

List the place interventions that you think would be helpful in each of your different high-risk situations.

	High-risk situation 1	High-risk situation 2	High-risk situation 3	High-risk situation 4
Place intervention 1				
Place intervention 2				
Place intervention 3				

ACTION ITEM 8.3

Chapter Summary and Roadmap

In this chapter you have identified the relevant place and activity variables that are relevant to your BFRB. You identified specific aspects of certain settings that make pulling or picking more likely to occur. You also were offered an array of different ways to change your behavior or your environment to make your BFRB less likely to happen. Review your list of place interventions and pick three that you are willing to try for this next week in the specific environments where they make sense.

Continue to fill out your Awareness Form for the following week and include interventions you used from the place domain

Please record every BFRB activity for the next week. Also, record the sensory, cognitive, affective, motor, and place interventions that you used. This will be your Awareness Form going forward. Use this form each week to record your BFRB urges and episodes.

Date/time	Location/activity	Behavior	Sensory interventions	Cognitive interventions	Affective interventions	Motor interventions	Place interventions	How long?

ACTION ITEM 8.4

ACTION ITEM 8.4

continued

Continue to work on your action items daily

Each day I will:

- ☐ continue to fill out my Awareness Form
- ☐ continue to edit and add to my Intervention Plan
- ☐ try incorporating some of the sensory, cognitive, affective, motor, and place interventions in my Intervention Plan to help me to change how I approach different places, activities, and high-risk environments

Part III

Lifestyle Changes and Maintenance of Recovery

9

The Importance of Self-Care

Overview

Self-care involves not only the care of your hair and skin, but also care of your well-being in general. Many people who engage in BFRBs become so focused on "perceived" imperfections or "problems," that they lose sight of the actual health of their skin and hair, as well as the state of their overall health. For example, participating in a healthy, daily skin and hair-care routine actually leads to improved conditions of the skin and hair. Thus, picking and pulling are discouraged and the benefits multiply. While picking and pulling might lead to mistaken impressions that improvements have been made to skin or hair, in reality they lead to damage and destruction. In this chapter we will introduce ideas to help you develop a healthier relationship with your skin and hair by replacing body-damaging beliefs and practices with beneficial ones. The result is not only directed toward reduced pulling or picking, but it also can improve your general well-being.

What You Need to Know

Hair and skin are not just ornamental features of our appearance, they are integral to its functioning, so it is necessary to keep these body parts healthy. You can do this through caring for them in new and healthier ways. We will provide a basic overview of the biology of hair and skin, as well as their growth characteristics, so that you can know what is normal as you continue on your journey to recovery. Let us start with the basics. Skin and hair are important body parts for your health and ultimate survival. They serve functions such as keeping organs in place, preventing loss of fluids, helping you to stay warm or cool, and protecting you from infection by germs and other toxins. Also, the skin helps to protect you by alerting you to pain and providing pleasurable sensations.

Skin consists of layers of tissues containing glands that produce sweat, oils, and wax, each of which serves necessary and beneficial functions. The skin also contains millions of pores, which allow things to exit (e.g., sweat) and enter (e.g., bacteria) the body. An important function of the skin is to protect us from injury and to help ward off infection by preventing potentially harmful toxins from entering the body and reaching the bloodstream.

To perform these functions well, skin must be intact and healthy. When the skin is broken, scraped, or otherwise damaged, these functions can fail unless additional precautions are taken, like wearing a bandage or using an antiseptic ointment. Fortunately, skin has the ability to repair itself very quickly, if given the chance. To heal, your body transports blood and lymph to wounds to form scabs and fight infection. A scab is like a natural bandage that protects while the skin is healing underneath. Over time, scabs get smaller and smaller until they are shed from the body, when the skin has healed sufficiently. Picking scabs can leave your body vulnerable to invasion by harmful microbes, causing infection and leading to scarring and other forms of cosmetic damage. Squeezing pimples can traumatize underlying tissue, damage healthy skin, and drive infections deeper into the body.

Hair also provides numerous health benefits including some minor ones such as assisting in the regulation of our body's temperature, though the sparse hair of humans compared with other creatures makes that less important. In addition, eyelashes and eyebrows help keep sweat and other small bits of matter out of our eyes. Hair on our heads provides a partial barrier from the sun's rays, which can damage our scalp if we are exposed for extended periods of time. Hair, unlike skin, is not essential for living, as is illustrated by cases of people living with alopecia universalis, a medical condition that renders individuals totally hairless.

By understanding the important functions of your hair and your skin, we hope that you will appreciate the importance of ensuring the health of these important features. Also, we want you to shift your focus away from unhelpful beliefs which you may hold, such as: "Gray hairs are ugly and make me look old" or "Blackheads are disgusting and I have to get rid of all of them" and toward more helpful ones, such as: "My hair is not perfect, but it is a pretty color and I like the cut" or "My skin protects my body and I am so grateful for that." The goal is to come to appreciate the health of your hair and skin and to regard them in a positive way, with less criticism and negativity. Creating a healthy relationship with your hair and skin helps you to reduce harsh and unnecessary self-critical thoughts about your body, replacing them with compassionate and self-accepting ones. Ultimately, this shift in focus supports you in taking appropriate care of your body and in opposing the mistaken idea that you are "fixing a problem."

Anatomy of Skin

Believe it or not, your skin is the largest organ of your body. It consists of seven layers, of which the outermost layer, the layer that you can touch and see, defends you from contaminants such as bacteria and ultraviolet (sun ray) damage, and keeps the body hydrated. The second skin layer is thicker and stronger and is only found on the palms of hands and the soles of feet and helps those areas withstand friction. This next layer is a bit deeper and helps maintain suppleness and moisture by attaching different types of fats together to create a protective barrier. Below that is a layer of cells associated with the immune system that helps fight against infection and germs. In this next layer, the skin transforms sunlight into vitamin D. The deeper two layers of skin contain sensory neurons that help register pain and regulate temperature, among other things. In addition, these contain blood vessels, nerve endings, hair follicles, and sweat glands.

Cells in the uppermost layer of your skin are constantly being sloughed off and replaced in a renewal process. This process is normal and natural in the cycle of skin. The deeper layers of the skin do not go through this cellular turnover and do not replace themselves as frequently. When wounds occur in this deeper layer, scar tissue forms and tends to remain for months, years, or sometimes permanently.

Anatomy of Hair

Your hair consists of two distinct parts: the follicle and the hair shaft. The follicle is the essential mechanism for growing hair and creating new cells. This is embedded in your skin and is not removed when your hair is extracted. The hair bulb, a fleshy structure at the base of most hairs, often misidentified as "the follicle," is of special interest to many people who pull their hair. The shaft consists of cells that are not living. Each hair on your body has a nerve ending (which is why you can feel a sensation as a hair is pulled out), a blood vessel to nourish the hair (which is why you can sometimes see blood at the end of the hair when it is pulled out), and a muscle (which is why your hair can "stand on end" when you are cold or when you shiver).

Your hair actually begins to grow under your skin, in the follicle. During the first stage of growth, the anagen phase, the follicle pushes the hair through the skin making it visible and allowing it to grow for up to three to five years at a rate of up to one centimeter each month. Every person has a different anagen phase, some shorter and some longer. People with longer anagen phases are able to grow very long hair, while people with short growth phases typically have short hair because there is less time for growth.

The next stage, the catagen phase, is short, about ten to fourteen days, where the hair follicle shrinks, cuts off blood flow from the body, and causes the follicle to die, thus allowing the hair to eventually fall out. During this time, the hair remains in place, but is held in the skin very tenuously. These hairs fall out easily, with slight tugs from hair brushing, washing, or even sleeping. These hairs sometimes remain in place throughout the third phase of the hair cycle.

The third phase of the hair cycle is the telogen phase, which is essentially a dormant phase for the hair follicle as it prepares to grow a new hair. This phase lasts approximately one to four months, after which the follicle is renewed and prepares to grow a new hair. At any given moment, 10 to 15 percent of hairs on a person's body are in this phase. Have you ever noticed that some hairs fall out more easily than others and have a very small, dark bulb? Chances are that these hairs are in the telogen phase of development and are preparing to fall out.

On average, humans will shed about one hundred hairs each day, mostly those that are in the third phase. When hairs are pulled out during the growth phase (phase 1), new hairs immediately begin growing, replacing the ones that were pulled out. When hairs are pulled while in the resting phase, it can be weeks or months before new hair begins to grow, depending on where those hairs are in the telogen phase. New hairs will not begin to grow until they naturally enter the growth phase. Fortunately, each hair on our bodies is on a different growth cycle, or else we would shed all of our hair at the same time.

A common fear is that hair will not regrow as a result of pulling. In most cases, hair will eventually grow back, once the telogen phase ends and the anagen phase begins. There are, however, cases where follicles stop producing hairs after repetitive trauma to the follicle, such as in hair pulling disorder. This may be particularly true for eyebrows and eyelashes. Such cases are rare and usually occur only after years of pulling. Know that more than likely, your hair will regrow if given adequate time to recover.

Anatomy of Nails

It is common for people with a BFRB to engage in other related body focused behaviors such as nail biting, nail picking, cuticle biting, and cuticle picking. Because nail biting and picking are common forms of BFRBs (estimates are about one in ten adults, and a greater proportion is likely among children and adolescents), there is a good chance that you have engaged in this behavior.

Fingernails and toenails are comprised of tissue called keratin, which is no longer living tissue. Fingernails and toenails are important because they help us to perform tasks – they serve as tools for gripping items, as scratching tools, and as protection for the tissue under the nail. Nails also serve to recognize sensations such as pain to prevent damage to the toe or fingers.

Repeated trauma to your nails from excessive biting or picking can cause distortions to their health and appearance causing ridges, discolorations, and unusual shapes.

Managing Damaged Skin, Hair, and Nails

Despite the ultimate damage to the hair, skin, or nails many people believe that their BFRB is helping them in some way. In other words, it is common to believe that picking and pulling is serving a useful purpose by correcting some existing problem. One possible result of picking or pulling can be a feeling of accomplishment or satisfaction, even after doing notable damage to the hair or skin. Is this a familiar feeling for you?

We want you to understand that picking and pulling do not solve any of the problems that you may think they solve. In fact, there are well-supported ways to address hair and skin issues that do not require any pulling or picking. For example, acne is better treated by dermatologist-recommended skin care regimens, as opposed to picking the affected skin. In fact, picking and squeezing blemishes makes acne worse, not better.

Healthy hair routines can provide similar benefits for improving a variety of hair concerns. If you tend to have dry hair, leaving conditioner on your hair and wrapping your hair in a towel for a period of time (thirty minutes to one hour) especially during high-risk times, can lead to softer and more hydrated hair. Not only can this discourage hair pulling, but it can also provide hydration and improve the hairs' appearance. Under-eye moisturizers or petroleum jelly can provide similar benefits for the brow or eyelashes. Dying hair that is gray can reduce triggers to pull. Managing any cosmetic hair removal can be put into the hands of professional stylists, dermatologists, or aestheticians.

Similarly, applying lotion or oil to skin in the morning or before bedtime can moisturize the skin and reduce dry, scaly patches. It also sends a message of "self-care" to you, rather than a "need to fix." Medicated ointments applied to damaged skin serve similar functions by reducing skin irritation, dryness, and pimple breakouts. Filing nails, clipping cuticles, and getting regular manicure/pedicures can keep nails in good condition to reduce uneven, jagged, dry nails/cuticles, and prevents unnecessary attention to these areas as well. The goals are to reduce triggers for pulling and picking and to accomplish desired outcomes in healthy, nondamaging ways. Self-care activities allow you to improve the look and feel of hair, skin, and nails while reducing potential triggers at these sites. Next, we will explore ideas about self-care that are not limited to skin, hair, and nails. Instead, they involve taking care of yourself as a whole person, on a daily basis, and focus on tending to your broader physical and emotional needs, leading to a richer, more fulfilling life (action item 9.1).

Identify relevant hair, skin, and nail care routines that you might employ to reduce triggers, and improve the health of your hair, skin, and nails

Take a moment to read through the following self-care routines that might help to improve the look, feel, and health of your hair, skin, and nails. Put a check mark next to the ones that you would like to try.

For Hair:

- ☐ Use a conditioner and leave it in your hair while in a towel for one hour at night.
- ☐ Brush your hair for ten minutes at night.
- ☐ Get your hair trimmed frequently to reduce split ends.
- ☐ Get your hair colored at a salon or with a home kit to color any off-color hair.
- ☐ Get a keratin treatment to tame coarse, curly hair.
- ☐ Purchase a soft, round brush to us to reduce hair breakage while styling.
- ☐ Wash hair at least every other day to reduce feelings of dirtiness or tackiness which can lead to pulling.
- ☐ Put petroleum jelly on your lashes and brows.
- ☐ Use eyelash serum to improve lash growth and strength.
- ☐ Take hair-growth vitamins to improve hair health.

For Skin:

- ☐ Moisturize both in the morning and at night with a pleasant-smelling lotion.
- ☐ Use blemish spots to cover any acne breakouts.
- ☐ Get a professional facial to take care of extractions.
- ☐ Take a hot bath with soothing, nourishing bath salts.
- ☐ See a dermatologist about acne or any other dermatological conditions.
- ☐ Put on a soothing face mask to improve skin health and moisture.
- ☐ Use under-eye patches for puffy eyes or to just moisturize this fragile skin.
- ☐ Take biotin and collagen to improve skin health.
- ☐ Drink lots of water each day.

For Nails:

- ☐ Get a professional manicure and pedicure on a regular basis.
- ☐ Use cuticle oil/cream to reduce dryness, hangnails.
- ☐ Use manicure gloves at night while watching television or when going to bed to soften skin on the hands and fingers.
- ☐ File fingernails regularly to reduce rough edges or smooth breaks.
- ☐ Take supplements to improve nail health.

Self-Care in General

Healthy Eating Habits

Your skin, hair, and nails (as well as important neurotransmitters such as serotonin and dopamine) gain nutrients needed to thrive from the foods that you eat. Eating a nutritious, balanced diet benefits hair, skin, and nails, as well as your entire body. Unhealthy eating practices can contribute to weight gain, lethargy, poor digestion, poor immune function, bouts of fatigue, decreased ability to problem-solve, irritability, and interference with pleasurable activities. Improving your diet can help to boost your mood, increase your confidence, and improve your overall health and wellness. Some people report that their BFRB is more severe when they eat a diet high in sugar and carbohydrates. Although there is no scientific evidence for this, it may be true for some individuals (action item 9.2).

Identify things that you might want to change about your diet

Review the following list of dietary changes and check the ones that you would like to implement going forward.

- ☐ Reduce fast food intake.
- ☐ Eat more vegetables.
- ☐ Eat more fruit.
- ☐ Eat less sugar (refined sugar such as is found in cookies, cake, and processed foods).
- ☐ Reduce or cut out sweets.
- ☐ Take a healthy lunch to work instead of dining out.
- ☐ Eat dinner earlier in the evening.
- ☐ Cut out late-night snacking.
- ☐ Make a fruit/vegetable smoothie.
- ☐ Do not snack between meals.
- ☐ Reduce intake of fried foods.
- ☐ Eat more whole foods, fewer processed foods.

Satisfying Sleep

Many people report pulling or picking around bedtime which can delay getting to sleep by minutes or by hours for some people. Lack of sleep as well as a reduction in sleep quality can cause irritability, fatigue, and decreased ability to focus the following day. Good sleep habits including a consistent bedtime and bedtime routine can help. Other factors that can impact sleep are viewing screens (phones, computers, tablets) before bedtime. The backlight from these devices interferes with production of melatonin, a hormone that assists in helping us fall asleep and maintaining good sleep quality. Having a solid bedtime routine that includes a reduction in screentime before bed, increased exercise during the day, limiting caffeine intake, going to bed at about the same time each night, and reducing alcohol consumption can help to regulate and improve sleep duration and quality. In addition, consider adding "wind down time" each evening prior to bedtime, such as a taking a warm bath, reading a book or magazine, applying scented lotion to the body, or engaging in one of the healthy skin or hair routines mentioned earlier in this chapter (action item 9.3).

ACTION ITEM 9.3

Identify things you can do to improve your sleep duration and quality

Take a moment to read through the following bedtime routines that might help to improve your sleep quality and duration. Put a check mark next to the ones that you would like to try.

- ☐ Remove all screens from the bedroom.
- ☐ Turn off the TV at least one hour before bedtime.
- ☐ Bathe before bed.
- ☐ If reading, using an electronic reader, turn off the blue backlight.
- ☐ Read a book before bed (use BFRB interventions if you engage in your BFRB while reading).
- ☐ Meditate before going to sleep.
- ☐ No caffeine after 2 PM.
- ☐ Get regular exercise.
- ☐ Do not eat within two hours of going to bed.
- ☐ Use a lavender pillow spray or room spray.
- ☐ Reduce alcohol intake.
- ☐ Practice deep breathing in bed.

Increasing Exercise

We have all heard that consistent exercise is good for us, but what you may not know is that exercise can also have direct benefits on your BFRB. Most people lead more-or-less sedentary lifestyles and simply do not get enough exercise. Sitting still for long periods of time provides opportunities for your hands to be free and to roam over your hair, skin, and nails searching for targets to attack. Further, insufficient physical exercise impedes the discharge of pent-up energy and limits opportunities for deep breathing, muscle activation, sensory stimulation, the release of endorphins, and physical stimulation. Increasing the amount of daily exercise can help reduce BFRB urges, satisfy the need for sensory stimulation, improve sleep, and positively affect mood and self-confidence. If you cringe at the thought of exercise, consider trying something different, perhaps a mild form of exercise that you may never have tried before, and start with manageable amounts of it until you are ready to add more (action item 9.4).

ACTION ITEM 9.4

Identify behavioral changes that could help you to get more exercise

Review the following list of behavioral changes involving exercise and check the ones that you would like to try.

- ☐ Go for a walk after dinner.
- ☐ Make exercise social, for example, meet a friend for a walk, at the gym, or at an exercise class.
- ☐ Lift weights several times a week to increase muscle strength and mass.
- ☐ Park further away from your destination to force you to have to walk.
- ☐ Take the stairs whenever possible.
- ☐ Join a gym or club for exercise and for socializing.
- ☐ Dance to music that you love.
- ☐ Spend a day in the yard gardening.
- ☐ Go for a walk after lunch.
- ☐ Check out training apps on your phone to see if there are any you might like to try.

Regulation of Emotions

Every day you likely experience many emotions and managing these emotions can be difficult. For many people, their BFRB becomes more severe during times of emotional upheaval. Therefore, one key to managing your BFRB is to manage your emotions as effectively as possible. We will review some skills to help you manage difficult emotions with the goal of reducing the role of your BFRB during challenging times. One of the more commonly reported emotional states conducive to pulling or picking is boredom. How can you deal with boredom? Make a list of things you like to do, as well as tasks that you need to do (a "to-do list"). The truth is, there are very few times in life where we legitimately have "nothing to do." Perhaps feeling bored for you is when you feel like "I do not have anything going on right now that I want to do." Making this list and keeping it in a place that is easily accessible at all times allows you to find "something to do" when you feel bored. Picking and pulling can feel "rewarding" or "gratifying" because in some ways you feel like you are "taking care of a problem." Having a list of real-life problems that need solving such as: cleaning out your junk drawer, organizing your purse, or taking out the trash can give you purpose that leads to actual, lasting satisfaction rather than feelings of momentary happiness followed by frustration and guilt. An important skill for emotion regulation is to develop plans to reduce boredom through constructive action. Next, we will discuss a number of other techniques to help you manage difficult emotions.

Self-Compassion

Mindful self-compassion is an approach to help you to have a more positive relationship with yourself. You are probably aware of the "voice" in your head that talks to you all day, the one that narrates your life. If this voice were a real person who followed you around all day and said those things, how would you feel about them? Would you like this person? Would you want to tell them to "get lost"? If the answer is anything but positive, welcome to humanity. Most people report that the voice in their head can be critical, negative, anxiety inducing, or just annoying. Self-compassion is an approach to help you to change this experience, to help this voice to become kinder and more supportive. It seems that people with a BFRB may engage in even more self-criticism than people who do not have a BFRB, leading to self-blame, self-criticism, and negative self-judgment. All of these can contribute to low self-esteem and low self-confidence, conditions that are common in people with BFRBs (Stemberger et al., 2000). As we talked about in Chapter 1, using the "best friend" technique when talking to yourself about your BFRB is key. We also want you to think about using these types of thoughts, those that you would say to your best friend in other, more general circumstances. Clinical experience suggests that people with BFRBs tend to have high expectations for themselves and tend to be quite perfectionistic about many aspects of their life. It is easy to get down on oneself when things are not going according to plan. Remember to ask yourself: "What would I say to my best friend if they were experiencing the exact same thing?" In general, people tend to be nicer to others than they are to themselves. Giving yourself the same consideration and kind words that you would give to a friend is an important step toward healthy self-care and therefore an important step on your journey to recovery. What do you give yourself a hard time about? Other than your BFRB, are there things that you criticize yourself for? What do you say to yourself in these situations? Just as you did in Chapter 1, make a list of the things that you say to yourself, then go back and change them to be what you would say to your best friend. What would those words be? Practice using these statements instead of the harsh ones, see how it feels. In the beginning, it will feel really strange, like you are "lying" to yourself. Keep practicing until those words feel like true words. Give this some time. As you know, old habits take time to change, and this is no different.

Relaxation

Tension or stress is a common experience reported by people before or while engaging in their BFRB. Tension can be physical, mental, and emotional. As a result, relaxation techniques can be very helpful in your efforts to combat BFRB urges. There are three relaxation approaches we want to highlight here: progressive muscle relaxation, mindful body scan, and breathing retraining.

Progressive Muscle Relaxation (PMR)

PMR is a process where attention is paid systematically to the tensing and relaxing of different muscle groups in the body. To do this you will want to lie down in a comfortable place where you will not be disturbed for five to twenty minutes. You will want to start at the feet and work your way up your body to different muscle groups. Start by clenching the muscles of your feet and holding it for five seconds, then relax. Do this again and hold for five to ten seconds. Notice the difference between how your muscles feel when they are tense and when they are relaxed. Move to your legs, tense the muscles of your legs and hold it for five to ten seconds, then repeat. Continue to tense and release different muscle groups moving up from your legs to your hips and stomach, to your hands, arms, neck, and shoulders, and finally to the face and head. For each muscle group practice tensing and releasing twice, noticing the different feelings between the two. After you have completed all muscle groups, notice if any muscles are still tense and, if so, go back and tense and release a few more times in those areas.

Mindful Body Scan (MBS)

MBS is another useful technique that, like PMR, helps to raise awareness of the tension that is held in various muscle groups as well as of other sensations and subtle movements in those muscles. MBS is designed to help you to observe and label varieties of bodily sensations, as they occur, to increase mindful awareness while letting go of judgment or actions to alter these sensations. This approach can be particularly helpful if you experience tingling, itching, burning, pressure, or more loosely defined "urges" as part of your BFRB experience. Observing bodily sensations while in a relaxed state can be enormously helpful to allow for an array of experiences to occur within one's awareness, without any action at all. In other words, you can learn to notice and observe sensations or urges, while not responding to them at all. To practice MBS, simply get into a comfortable, relaxed position and close your eyes. Focus on your breathing and on letting go of tension in your body. Just notice what you feel: Do you feel itches, a desire to move, hunger, thirst, or a slight headache? Just notice. Try not to do anything to change these sensations, just notice them and maybe describe how they feel. Try not to use any judgments such as "This is bad" or "I hate this sensation," but instead focus on how it feels, as if you have never felt this sensation before. As you practice these skills, you can check in with your body at any time during the day such as at work, while driving, or watching TV. Begin to notice how your body feels throughout the day, without any judgment.

Breathing Retraining

Other approaches to relaxation of the body include those that alter your patterns of breathing. Deep, purposeful breathing can, when practiced, alter breathing throughout the day, even when you are not practicing it or even focused on it. In addition, breathing to calm the body and nervous system is a tool that can be used when you are feeling stressed, overwhelmed, or when facing an urge to either pull or pick. Probably the simplest and most helpful breathing technique is to inhale deeply for four counts, then take one more, quick sip of air to fill your lungs completely, then release all of the breath for at least six counts. Repeat this five to ten times each day. Extending your exhale so it takes longer than your inhale activates the parasympathetic nervous system which is the relaxation and restorative system of your body that promotes a feeling of calm when it is activated.

Mindfulness Approaches

Now that you know how to relax your body, we want to address techniques for quieting your mind. If your body is trying to relax, but your mind is racing with stressful thoughts, it is going to be hard to maintain a state of relaxation. The next skill we will cover is "thought watching," and it will help to calm your mind. The purpose of thought watching is to help you observe and learn about your thoughts, without responding to them. As with the relaxation exercises described above, this one is usually done while you are sitting comfortably or lying down. Focus on your breath and allow your mind to settle and your body to relax. While you are focusing on the breath, notice what thoughts are occurring as you simply focus on your breathing. It is likely that your thinking will wander and that extraneous thoughts will intrude into your consciousness. When that happens, gently return to focus on your breathing and return to the present moment. It is normal for your mind to wander, so do not become frustrated, this is expected. What is curious is *where* your mind wanders to; what thoughts emerge when you focus on your breath? Each time your mind wanders, be aware of it, notice where the mind went, then gently return to your breath and to the present moment. People typically report that the mind tends to wander to predictable places, such as thinking about the past, worrying about the future, judging themselves harshly, or simply "wandering." Notice these wanderings and make a mental note of them, so that you can be more aware of them in the future. Ultimately, the goal is to be able to identify when the mind wanders and to return it to the present through the breath. The process of returning one's focus to the present eliminates any power that you might have given to that thought. Thoughts can lead us away from what we are doing in the present, they can carry us into experiencing worry and anxiety. Simply noticing when the mind wanders and returning it to the present, without engaging these thoughts, is incredibly helpful for regulating one's emotions. This exercise should take about ten minutes. Over time and with practice, you can learn to observe thoughts and other internal experiences without responding to or judging them, allowing you to live more in the present moment where you can be intentional about your actions. Mindfulness-based practices such as this can have a positive impact on your well-being in general, as well as on your BFRB, specifically.

Practicing a variety of positive self-care techniques will provide you with important resources for managing your BFRB by helping you create a healthier relationship with your hair and skin, as well as with your broader life. In addition, these techniques can effectively boost your self-esteem, increase your ability to cope with stress, provide a routine that encourages beneficial movement, increase mindful awareness, improve distress tolerance, and improve emotion regulation skills. These techniques will help you reach your goals with your BFRB program. Management of BFRBs is a challenging enterprise and self-care of hair, skin, and the body and mind are important steps on the journey to recovery.

ACTION ITEM 9.5

Identify techniques for improving your ability to regulate emotions

Check off the strategies that you would like to try to help you with regulating your emotions.

- ☐ self-compassion
- ☐ relaxation
- ☐ progressive muscle relaxation
- ☐ mindful body scan
- ☐ breathing retraining
- ☐ practice mindfulness

Medications and Nutraceuticals

We are often asked about medications and nutraceuticals (supplements) that may help to reduce the occurrence of BFRBs. The truth is that no psychiatric medications have been consistently found to help with the frequency or intensity of BFRBs. That said, if a person is struggling with depression or anxiety, and pulling or picking is worsened by feelings of sadness or anxiety, antidepressant/antianxiety medications (typically selective serotonin reuptake inhibitors [SSRIs] or serotonin-norepinephrine reuptake inhibitors [SNRIs]) might be able to help. However, these medications alone do not consistently reduce BFRB symptomatology in nondepressed and nonanxious people. Memantine, a drug used for people with Alzheimer's disease was tested on a group of people with trichotillomania and skin picking disorder and results showed that 60.5 percent of participants in the memantine group were "much or very much improved," compared to 8.3 percent in the placebo group (Grant et al., 2023). We recommend talking with a knowledgeable psychiatrist who can help guide you on making medication decisions.

There is one nutraceutical option that has shown to help with reducing urges to pull hair or pick skin. N-acetylcysteine (NAC) has shown promise in clinical studies for reducing symptomatology in people with hair pulling disorder (Grant et al., 2009). Results showed that 56 percent of people who took NAC reduced their pulling as compared to 16 percent of those taking a placebo. There were no significant, negative side effects demonstrated in those taking the NAC suggesting that it is potentially a good option to help support those making therapeutic efforts. We like to think of medication and nutraceutical supplementation as one piece of the puzzle and a potentially helpful one for some people. Coupled with the efforts you are making throughout this workbook, these additions could add positively to your overall approach and increase your chances for ultimate success.

Chapter Summary and Roadmap

In this chapter we have suggested ways for you to keep your hair, skin, and nails healthy. Often BFRBs are attempts to "fix" a perceived problem. If you can find healthier ways to address things that bother you about your hair and skin in ways that do not cause harm to your body, that would be great! We also reviewed a number of self-care approaches that are designed to help improve your life in general, including sleep, nutrition, exercise, and emotional well-being. Now, your plan includes specific techniques to help you with your BFRB (e.g., to address cues and triggers for pulling or picking), as well as ways to care for yourself in general that will help to improve your BFRB in other ways. We find that addressing BFRBs on multiple levels tends to have the greatest likelihood for success.

Identify lifestyle changes and add them to your BFRB Journey Plan here

Each day I will:

- ☐ continue to fill out my Awareness Form
- ☐ continue to edit and add to my Intervention Plan
- ☐ continue to incorporate the sensory, cognitive, affective, motoric, and place interventions in my Intervention Plan to help me change how I approach different places, activities, and high-risk environments
- ☐ add self-care activities into my daily routine

10

Putting It All Together to Move Forward

We have covered a lot of ground in this workbook and this final chapter will help you pull it all together so that you can move forward with your own comprehensive plan. You have learned a lot in the last nine chapters and there is a lot of information to digest. We have encouraged you to proceed slowly and to revise your plan often and as needed. In that spirit, we would like to briefly review some of the key points from earlier chapters before you move on.

Looking Back

After reading this book and filling out the action items, we are confident that you have spent some valuable time thinking about your BFRB and making sense of it. Hopefully, you have realized that having a BFRB is not your fault, that you did not cause it and that you did not choose to have this problem in your life. You understand that hair pulling and skin picking represent your efforts to take care of yourself, often by regulating internal states in a variety of different circumstances. Thinking about your BFRB in rational and measured ways is an important step in learning to effectively manage these problems. You learned a lot about BFRBs including how they are defined, how common they are, and the multitude of ways they can meet a person's individual needs, and you understand that many things about these perplexing disorders are still unknown. Importantly, now you better understand how BFRBs impact your life: emotionally, physically, psychologically, socially, and functionally. Understanding the effects of having a BFRB helps to increase motivation and helps make the case for initiating change. A common and profound result of the BFRB experience is the shame that most people report. Often, people feel misunderstood and even blamed for having a BFRB, and that can undermine their efforts to make the necessary changes that are required for them to heal. It can be easy to get stuck in feelings of anger as if your situation has unfairly fallen on you: "Why do I have this terrible problem and other people do not even understand how awful it is?" This is a sentiment that we have heard expressed in many ways. We hope that the action items in this book have helped you to reduce the shame that usually accompanies a BFRB. We encourage you to revisit the action items in Chapter 1 that specifically address the shame in your BFRB "story" (action items 1.1 and 1.4). As you progress along your journey to recovery, your feelings will change as will your BFRB story. Sometimes it is helpful to revisit old stories to see how your narrative has changed over time and how healing has taken place. Ultimately, we hope that you move away from anger and frustration toward self-acceptance and self-compassion.

Along this journey you also learned about some myths and misconceptions about BFRBs that are just plain incorrect. Having an accurate and complete foundation for understanding these problems arms you with knowledge and the power to challenge untruths when you are faced with them, whether they are generated by adopting other people's beliefs or through your own thinking and beliefs. You learned how you can want to make major changes, but might not yet be ready to make the changes in your daily routine that are required to reach your goal. The action items were designed to help you identify where you are regarding readiness for change and how to take steps toward making the necessary modifications to your routine if that is needed.

We have encouraged you to explore your expectations for therapy, the goals you have set for yourself and the importance of timing in your efforts. Setting realistic expectations is a key component to successful behavior change. Have you set realistic expectations and are your goals achievable? Stephen R. Covey, in his book, *The 7 Habits of Highly Effective People* (1991) used the phrase "Fast is slow and slow is fast," which refers to effective goal-setting and behavior change. What this means is that when we shoot for making fast change (e.g., going from limited physical activity to getting at least an hour of brisk exercise every day), change often never happens at all or only happens for a short period of time. Alternately, setting a more realistic goal (e.g., exercising thirty minutes, four times a week) can result in a greater likelihood of success. In other words, accept the possibility that big changes will take time and that small, daily changes will help you reach your goals faster and more effectively. James Clear, in his book *Atomic Habits: An Easy & Proven Way to Build Good Habits & Break Bad Ones* (2018), talks about the power of making tiny, "micro" changes daily, resulting in grand-scale outcomes later. Again, think about your journey as an accumulation of many tiny changes and decisions that ultimately maximize your chance for success, rather than a big change that you will achieve quickly. We encourage you to identify the small, concrete changes that you are willing and able to do, and to focus on doing those things consistently.

Always remember that this process will certainly not progress without a hitch. You must now be fully aware that the journey toward significant behavior change can be a bumpy road at best, filled with potholes and other impediments that will threaten your progress. However, these bumps are inevitable parts of life. Learning to cope with disappointments and setbacks is important for many reasons: it helps you to problem-solve your way back to productive activity, it builds resilience, and it helps you to develop compassion toward yourself in the face of disappointment. Ultimately it will allow you to then move toward your goals with grace and insight.

We have asked you to imagine what your life would be like with the ability to manage your BFRB. How will you manage difficult times and stressful days? How will you fall asleep at night or watch television while maintaining your efforts to manage your BFRB? What would BFRB management actually look like in real life practice? Hopefully you now have a good idea of what this would look like.

Chapters in Review

Chapter 1 is perhaps the most important chapter in this workbook, because it sets the stage for the behavior changes that will follow. In that chapter you learned to:

- confront aspects of your belief system,
- explore your struggle with your BFRB, and
- examine the beliefs prevalent in our society; those are often the harmful ones.

Remember that this work will not produce lasting success in one week or even two, it is your life's work and will be constantly evolving and developing. We hope that Chapter 1 has started you on your journey to recovery from the blame, shame, and guilt that often plagues people with a BFRB.

Chapter 2 begins the formulation of the concepts used to create the ComB approach, pinpointing the five common domains that underlie BFRBs and helping you see how each one might apply to you:

- You learned the five domains – sensory, cognitive, affective, motor, and environmental (place) variables that lead people to pick or pull and reinforce them for doing so.
- Through self-monitoring you have increased your knowledge of the internal and external cues, triggers, and reinforcing factors that influence *your* BFRB.

In addition, we hope that through the daily monitoring of your behavior and mindfulness practices, you also learned the conditions under which your BFRB occurs and are able to anticipate its occurrence even before it starts. This allows you to make specific adjustments that reduce the likelihood of picking or pulling. We have attempted to drive home the point that you are unlikely to change a behavior pattern if you are not aware that it is happening. Awareness is critical for behavior change. Awareness plus the utilization of specific interventions (skills used in specific situations) is the absolute recipe for success.

Chapter 3 helped you to integrate information that you have learned into a detailed, descriptive summary of your BFRB:

- You identified relevant cues, triggers, and reinforcing factors for your BFRB. In other words, this chapter helped you to better understand your hair pulling and skin picking patterns – the what, when, where, and how of your BFRB.
- You identified different functions that your BFRB serves in your life, the "why" of your BFRB.

The emphasis on BFRBs as "functional behaviors" is a reminder that people do not engage in behaviors repeatedly that do not serve them in some way. Uncovering how your BFRB serves you, even in very subtle ways, allows you to find alternate strategies for getting those needs met, in ways that do not cause physical or psychological harm. Seeing your behavior as functional and in some ways serving your needs, though unwanted and often hated, will help reduce some of the shame and guilt that often is associated with BFRBs. Understanding that "I pick my skin because I feel like it helps me to get rid of that rough sensation that I cannot stand," or "It enables me to think through my troubles more effectively," or "It helps me to wind down from a hard day," or "My pimples will heal better if I squeeze something out of them," and similar facilitating thoughts and beliefs, somehow makes skin picking seem less diabolical. Knowing the "why" also reveals pathways to healing because it allows you to then find alternate ways to "feel smoothness," or "handle life's troubles," or "wind down from a hard day," or "help heal my pimples." Chapter 3 also reviewed some common obstacles to success with BFRB change (emotions, cognitive, and perfectionistic expectations), and provided helpful pathways through these common but stubborn obstacles. Hopefully, you were able to identify things that might have stood in your way in the past or that currently stand in the way of a successful journey forward. Knowing the answer does not always mean that we make the right decision, does it? Understanding that BFRB recovery is a fraught process allows self-compassion and self-forgiveness to emerge, and ultimately allows you to forgive yourself for being the "perfectly imperfect" person that you are.

Chapters 4 through 8 focused on active measures that you can take to manage your BFRB. We introduced an array of specific interventions to consider:

- You identified the five domains that are active for you in your life.
- Based upon your relevant domains, we presented an array of potentially helpful interventions to construct your Intervention Plan.

- You created an Intervention Plan that identifies key strategies for success in managing your BFRB.
- You tried some interventions within each domain to identify ones that work for you.
- At the end of Chapter 8, you should have finalized a plan for the situations where your BFRB is most active.

We hope that you were able to identify a variety of interventions that could be helpful in specific high-risk situations so that you now have tools for success in resisting triggers and getting your needs met in healthy and sustainable ways.

Chapter 9 was all about self-care. Throughout this chapter you learned about:

- healthy skin and hair care
- healthy diet and exercise
- self-compassion
- relaxation and other mindfulness approaches
- medication or nutraceutical supplementation

All of these tools will help your overall BFRB journey. When you are flying in an airplane you definitely want a competent pilot in control (you with your Intervention Plan), but you also want a plane that has been well maintained with oil changes, system checks, routine maintenance, and replacement of old parts (your healthy lifestyle). The routine maintenance is arguably as important as the competent pilot. The best pilot in the world can have trouble flying a poorly maintained airplane. We hope that you have incorporated many of these lifestyle changes into your daily routine, so that your intervention plan can be as successful as possible.

Creating a Plan to Move Forward

So, what's next? How do you integrate all of this information into a coherent plan forward? We recommend that you revisit the action items in Chapters 1 through 3 to make sure that you have identified all the relevant influences on your BFRB, both internal and external. Just as seasons change, so do the factors that influence BFRB performance. Different seasons of life also bring different challenges. Return to this workbook in the future, to update the information and to reconsider what factors are contributing to persistent BFRB occurrences. Consider a woman who had learned to manage her BFRB well, but then became pregnant and had her first child. Faced with a whole new set of joys, hormones, stressors, daily (and nightly) alterations in her routine and so on, she regressed backwards into former BFRB habits. Any major life changes can provide a great opportunity to assess the impact of the new factors that impact a BFRB. Armed with this new information (e.g., late-night nursing as a new time for BFRB activity), this woman might then review specific interventions in Chapters 4 through 8, to help develop an intervention plan for this new high-risk situation. She might also revisit her daily self-help plan and consider how, given her new circumstance, she could best attend to her current needs.

We encourage you to do the same, to view your journey not as a quick sight-seeing excursion, but as a lifelong journey to experience the world in new and satisfying ways. Some trips are going to be more pleasant or more challenging than others. For example, a trip to visit challenging family members will likely have a different feel than spending a week at a spa in a beautiful mountain retreat. Many factors will dictate how you approach each of these trips. Likewise, your BFRB journey will also have some easier and some more challenging elements over the years. Use what you have learned in this workbook as your roadmap, but also understand that there will be new circumstances that will require adjustments along the way. We encourage you to be patient and to view challenges and setbacks as normal and unavoidable experiences along the way. Remember, small victories every day can result in a total transformation over time.

Coming Home

The vacation is over, now what? When you return home from a vacation, what happens? Maybe you talk about your trip, show pictures to friends and loved ones, post about your adventures, and so on, but how about this journey? Now that your trip is coming to a conclusion, what is next? Coming home can be sad, a relief, or anxiety-producing as you must return to daily life, work, and routine. Using our metaphor of your managing your BFRB being a journey or trip that you must prepare for, we realize that sometimes the hardest part of the trip is coming home. How do you integrate what you have learned into your life, for the long haul? We want you to integrate the things you have learned into your daily habits and routines so that you can be consistent going forward. Things might go well for a while and then you may be invited by your BFRB to go on another adventure. Know that slips (falling back into old habits) are normal and expected. Just as when we travel, we learn "tricks" that help us in the future (e.g., like how to pack for two weeks in a carry-on suitcase), you will learn BFRB "tricks" as well. Incorporate what works into your routine and know that you will add new habits later, as you grow and learn about yourself. Sometimes we forget what we have learned and have to go back and review, this is okay too! Remember, be gentle with yourself and try to view setbacks as opportunities to learn about yourself and what works for you. This journey with BFRBs is a lifetime journey, but you get wiser as you progress, learning how to manage difficult situations better, with patience and grace.

Maintenance

When you have identified the right combination of interventions and have mastered when to use them, we call this maintenance. Maintenance is the time where you are managing your BFRB through the use of interventions. As you progress in your management of your BFRB, things will get easier, your BFRB will reduce, and you may rely less on the interventions than you did at the start of this journey. We recommend using interventions pretty heavily until you have gone about a year feeling like your symptoms are pretty well managed. A year may seem like a long time, but all too often we see people abandoning their tools before they are ready, and they experience backsliding. If you find tools that work, continue to use them, forever if you need to. Typically, people do not have to hold onto all of their interventions forever. For example, if your interventions for your picking in the bathroom at night, in front of the mirror after a long day include dimming the lights, removing needles, covering the mirror, and limiting time spent in the bathroom, you may use all of these for a year or two. After you feel like you have eliminated picking in this environment, you might consider removing the cover from the mirror and allowing the lights to be a little brighter. You would likely not put needles back in the bathroom or go back to spending hours in this environment. You can practice eliminating interventions and see how you do. Are you able to be successful or do you need to put the interventions back in place? All of this is part of maintenance and learning what works for you as time goes on.

Conclusion

What we have learned in our work with thousands of clients for over thirty years is that there are many important elements in successful treatment. One key element is laying a proper foundation for change, which includes: gathering accurate information, helping to reduce shame, creating realistic expectations, learning to evaluate the details of your BFRB, and developing healthy life practices. There is a lot to a good, solid foundation! Let us begin with gathering accurate information. Reading this book has provided you with lots of important information. We encourage you to continue to learn and gather accurate information from reputable sources, such as the TLC Foundation for Body Focused Repetitive Behaviors (bfrb.org) and the International OCD Foundation (IOCDF.org). Continue your progress toward alleviating shame about having a BFRB and undoing negative learning experiences from your past. Shame disrupts efforts to make progress and weakens motivation. Shame fuels negative self-talk and fosters self-blame. Shame can cause you to feel powerless, while letting go of shame allows for your power to return. Remember that you are not alone. Many people share similar challenges and struggles. Work hard to create realistic expectations for yourself during each step of this journey and be kind to yourself, you deserve support from the person who is always with you – you. Be realistic. Developing small, attainable goals helps create feelings of success and cultivates the ability to move forward. Remember to maintain healthy lifestyle practices on a daily basis. These practices include beneficial routines such as increased sleep, improved exercise, positive skin- and haircare, as well as effective management of emotions. Continue to evaluate the unique factors that drive your BFRB and know that they may change with time as we all do.

We hope that this workbook has been helpful for learning effective tools to manage your BFRB. Sometimes books are not enough, and we understand that. In a compassionate, nonjudgmental manner you may want to seek additional forms of support and/or guidance. The TLC Foundation for BFRBs is an excellent source of information and support. They provide online support groups and have a list of providers in every state who have knowledge about treatment of BFRBs. You may also want to seek out some in-person support groups as well. Explore the options that exist for you to get the type of help that will resonate with you.

We hope this book has been effective in describing how your efforts to change are facilitated when you view your problems in a compassionate and nonjudgmental way. Furthermore, we have guided you in selecting precise interventions that are tailored to your unique needs as were identified in action items provided in earlier chapters. Focusing on the details of your BFRB and how it functions in your life can be a daunting process, so be prepared to take care of yourself as best you can while you are on this path. Having come this far, you are now prepared to move forward, not only armed with knowledge, but also with a clear perspective about what this process might entail. Knowing that you cannot expect perfection on this journey allows you to move through any hard times ahead effectively and successfully, without squandering your energies in frustration, anger, or self-judgment. We want you to thrive, knowing that you have the tools for success. Bon Voyage!

References

American Psychiatric Association (2022). *Diagnostic and Statistical Manual of Mental Disorders*, fifth edition. Arlington, VA: American Psychiatric Association.

Clear, J. (2018). *Atomic Habits: An Easy & Proven Way to Build Good Habits & Break Bad Ones*. New York: Penguin Random House.

Covey, S. R. (1991). *The Seven Habits of Highly Effective People*. Provo, UT: Covey Leadership Center.

Grant, J. E., Chesivoir, E., Valle, S., Ehsan D., & Chamberlain, S. (2023). Double-blind placebo-controlled study of memantine in trichotillomania and skin-picking disorder. *American Journal of Psychiatry, 180*(5), 348–356.

Grant, J. E., Odlaug, B. L., & Kim, S. W. (2009). N-acetylcysteine, a glutamate modulator, in the treatment of trichotillomania: A double-blind, placebo-controlled study. *Archives of General Psychiatry, 66*(7), 756–763.

Hayes, S. C., Luoma, J. B., Bond, F. W., Masuda, A., & Lillis, J. (2006). Acceptance and commitment therapy: Model, processes and outcomes. *Behaviour Research and Therapy, 44*(1), 1–25.

Keuthen, N. J., Altenberger, E. M., & Pauls, D. (2014). A family study of trichotillomania and chronic hair pulling. *American Journal of Medical Genetics, 165*(2), 167–174.

Lee, E. B., Homan, K. J., Morrison, K. L., Ong, C. W., Levin, M. E., & Twohig, M. P. (2020). Acceptance and commitment therapy for trichotillomania: A randomized controlled trial of adults and adolescents. *Behavior Modification, 44*(1), 70–91.

Lochner, C., du Toit, P. L., Zungu-Dirwayi, N., Marais, A., van Kradenburg, J., Seedat, S., & Stein, D. J. (2002). Childhood trauma in obsessive-compulsive disorder, trichotillomania, and controls. *Depression and Anxiety, 15*(2), 66–68.

Mansueto, C. S., & Rogers, K. E. (2012). Trichotillomania: Epidemiology and clinical characteristics. In Grant, J. E., Stein, D. J., Woods, D. W., & Keuthen, N. J. (eds.), *Trichotillomania, Skin Picking and Other Body Focused Repetitive Behaviors* (pp. 3–20). Arlington, VA: American Psychiatric Publishing.

Neff, K. (2011). *Self-Compassion: Stop Beating Yourself Up and Leave Insecurity Behind*. New York: William Morrow & Company.

Odlaug, B. L. & Grant, J. E. (2012). Pathologic skin picking. In Grant, J. E., Stein, D. J., Woods, D. W., & Keuthen, N. J. (eds.), *Trichotillomania, Skin Picking and Other Body Focused Repetitive Behaviors* (pp. 21-41). Arlington, VA: American Psychiatric Publishing.

Stemberger, R. M. T., Thomas, A. M., Mansueto, C. S., & Carter, J. G. (2000). Personal toll of trichotillomania: Behavioral and interpersonal sequelae. *Journal of Anxiety Disorders, 14*(1), 97-104.

Woods, D. W., Flessner, C. A., & Franklin, M. E. (2006). The Trichotillomania Impact Project (TIP): Exploring phenomenology, functional impairment, and treatment utilization. *Journal of Clinical Psychiatry, 67*(12), 1877-1888.

Index

ABC model of behavior change, 60, 64, 67–70
acceptance
   and cognitive flexibility, 117–118
   techniques, 139
   thoughts, 114
acceptance and commitment therapy (ACT), values and valued living, 121
action items
   overview, 6
   affective domain
      BFRB journey plan, 146
      changing your level of stimulation, 141
      choosing interventions, 142
      describing urges like a journalist, 131–132
      emotion management strategies, 137
      identifying relevant emotions, 135
      logging BFRB activity, 144
      urge surfing, 133
   BFRB journey checklist, 59
   cognitive domain
      adding strategies to intervention plan, 122
      BFRB journey plan, 126
      identifying and changing problematic thoughts, 114
      improving cognitive flexibility, 119–120
      logging BFRB activity, 123, 144
   completing your BFRB journey plan, 82
   envisioning the end of your story, 18
   exploring "best friend thoughts," 21–23
   goal setting, 29–30
   High-Risk Situation Form
      completing, 63–64
      example, 62
   identifying
      cognitive barriers to recovery, 79
      the functions of your BFRB, 71–72
      the impact of your BFRB, 13–15
      relevant As, Bs, and Cs, 69
      your SCAMP domains, 43–45
   learn about your behavior chains, 65–67
   listing
      the positives of your BFRB and possible alternatives, 73
      your SCAMP domains in order of relevance, 46

   mindfulness exercise, 57
   motor domain
      continue to work on action items daily, 157
      identify specific interventions to use, 153
      learn array of interventions, 152
      logging BFRB activity, 155–156
   place domain
      continue to work on action items daily, 171
      identifying
         interventions, 166–167
         relevant variables, 163–164
      logging BFRB activity, 169
   readiness assessment, 26–28
   recording BFRB activity, 48–49
   self-care
      behavioral changes involving exercise, 188
      emotion regulation techniques, 194
      healthy eating interventions, 184
      improving sleep duration and quality, 186
      lifestyle changes, 197
      relevant hair, skin, and nail care routines, 182
   sensory domain
      BFRB journey plan, 110
      intervention plan, 106
      logging BFRB activity, 107, 123, 144
      near senses, 105
      oral/taste, 99
      smell, 101
      sound, 103
      touch, 96
      vision, 89–91
   timing, 32–33
   writing your BFRB story, 16
   your BFRB journey, 35
affective domain, 40, 43–44
   overview, 127–129
   acceptance techniques, 139
   breathing and "best friend thoughts," 128
   choosing interventions, 142
   coping
      with difficult emotions, 136–138
      with distress, 129
   defusing the urge from the action, 130
   describing urges like a journalist, 131–132

Index

emotion regulation, 138
example interventions, 129
feeling over- or under-stimulated, 140-141
identifying difficult emotions, 134-136
learning to ignore an urge, 133
logging BFRB activity, 144
age of onset for BFRBs, average, 8
anxiety, commonly coexisting with BFRBs, 9
Atomic Habits: An Easy & Proven Way to Build Good Habits & Break Bad Ones (Clear), 200
awareness of behaviors
  overview, 37
  awareness enhancing tools, 150
  behavior chains, 40
  benefits for understanding BFRBs, 3, 19-20
  developing your BFRB profile, 47
  domains of relevance, 37-42
    see also SCAMP domains
  importance for recovery, 38, 42, 58
  increasing, 36-59
  mindfulness as strategy for gaining, 52, 53
  mindfulness exercise, 54-57
  patterns of behavior, 51-52
  recording BFRB activity, 48-49
  role of blockers, 148, 150

bathroom, potential role in BFRB activity, 159
behavior chains, learning about your, 65-67
behavior change
  ABC model, 60, 64, 67-70
  role of realistic expectations, 200
Behavior Therapy Center of Greater Washington, 37
"best friend thoughts," exploring, 21-23
BFRBs (body focused repetitive behaviors)
  overview, 7
  effects of, 11, 12, 13-14
  examples of, 7
  importance of understanding reasons for engagement in, 19
  potential triggers, 11
  prevalence, 10
  unknowns, 10
blockers, examples of, 148, 150, 152, 162
body scan, mindful, 191-192
breathing retraining, 192

change, readiness for, 25
Clear, James, *Atomic Habits: An Easy & Proven Way to Build Good Habits & Break Bad Ones*, 200
cognitive domain, 39, 43
  acceptance, 117-118
  acceptance thoughts, 114
  adding strategies to intervention plan, 122

categories of thought, 111
challenging unhelpful thoughts, 112-113
cognitive flexibility
  benefits of, 116-118
  learning how to improve, 119-120
identifying and changing problematic thoughts, 114
identifying different types of thoughts, 112
logging BFRB activity, 107, 123, 144
and pain management, 116-117
perfectionistic thinking, 115-116
resistance thoughts, 114
valued living, 121
competitive responses, expansion, 151
Comprehensive Behavioral (ComB) Model, development of, 37
Comprehensive Behavioral (ComB) Treatment of Body Focused Repetitive Behaviors: A Clinical Guide, 3
Covey, Stephen R., *The 7 Habits of Highly Effective People*, 200

defusion, 121, 130
depression, commonly coexisting with BFRBs, 9
dermatillomania, *see also* skin picking disorder (SPD), 8
distress, coping with, 129
DSM-5-TR (*Diagnostic and Statistical Manual of Mental Disorders*), inclusion of BFRBs in, 7

eating habits, healthy, 183
effects of BFRBs, 11, 12, 13-14
emotions
  coping with difficult emotions, 136-138
  emotion regulation, 138
  identifying difficult emotions, 134-136
"encouragers," 67
excoriation disorder, *see also* skin picking disorder (SPD), 8
expectations
  and goal setting, 27-30
  setting realistic expectations, 199-200

genetic basis of BFRBs, research into, 8
goal setting, expectations and, 27-30

habit reversal therapy, 150-151
The Habits of Highly Effective People (Covey), 221
hair
  anatomy, 178-179
  health, 176-177
  managing damage to, 180-181

Index

hair pulling disorder (HPD)
   inclusion in DSM-5, 7
   prevalence in adults, 9
healthy eating habits, 183

implements, role of in BFRB activity, 160-161
interventions
   affective domain, 127-146
   cognitive domain, 111-126
   motor domain, 147-157
   place domain, 158-171
   sensory domain, 85-110
   see also individual domains

lighting, potential role in BFRB activity, 160
locations, role of in BFRB activity, 159

Mansueto, Charles, 37
mindful body scan, 191-192
mindful self-compassion, 116, 189-190
mindfulness
   approaches, 192-193
   exercise
      script 1, 54, 55
      script 2, 56
   fundamental premise of, 52
   as strategy for gaining awareness of behaviors, 52, 53
motivation for change vs. readiness, 25
motor domain, 40-41, 44
   overview, 147-148
   awareness enhancing tools, 150
   blocker examples, 148, 150, 152
   expansion of competitive responses, 151
   focused and automatic styles of BFRB, 149-150
   habit reversal therapy, 150-151
   intervention examples, 152-153
   logging BFRB activity, 155-156
   postural change, 150
   and "trance-like state," 151
myths and misconceptions about BFRBs, 23-25

nails
   anatomy, 179
   managing damage to, 180-181
Neff, Kristin, 116
negative impact of BFRBs, examples of, 11, 12, 13-14

Obsessive Compulsive Disorder (OCD), relationship of BFRBs to, 7
oral behaviors, taste and, *see* taste and oral behaviors
other people's absence/presence, potential role in BFRB activity, 161-162

perfectionistic thinking, 115, 116
place domain, 41, 44
   overview, 158
   activities, 162
   bathroom, 159
   implements, 160-161
   intervention examples, 165-167
   lighting, 160
   other people's absence/presence, 161-162
   physical location, 159
   relevant variables, 163-164
   situational variables, 158
   time of day, 160
   using blockers, 162
prevalence of BFRBs, 10
puberty, 8
pulling it all together, 198-207
   creating a plan to move forward, 203-204
   key to successful treatment, 206, 207
   looking back, 198-200
   maintenance, 205-206
   review of chapters, 201, 203
   revisiting action items, 199
   setting realistic expectations, 199-200

readiness
   for change, motivation and, 25
   to overcome your BFRB, assessment of, 26-28
realistic expectations, role in successful behavior change, 200
recovery
   overview of how this book will help, 4
   importance of awareness of behaviors for, 38, 42, 58
   importance of understanding reasons for engagement in BFRBs, 19
   potential barriers to, 74-78
      cognitive impediments, 77-78, 79
      emotional obstacles, 74-76
   role of timing, 31
relapse prevention, 80, 81
relaxation, 191-194
   breathing retraining, 192
   mindful body scan, 191-192
   mindfulness approaches, 192-193
   progressive muscle relaxation, 191
resistance thoughts, 114
responses, competitive, 151

SCAMP domains
   overview, 37-38
   sensory, 38-39, 43
   cognitive, 39, 43
   affective, 40, 43-44

motor, 40-41, 44
place, 41, 44
identifying your domains, 43-45
internal vs. external, 42
listing in order of relevance to you, 46
see also individual domains
self-care, 175-197
  emotion regulation, 189, 194
  example
    dietary changes, 184
    routines, 182
  exercise, 187
  hair anatomy, 178-179
  hair and skin health, 176-177
  healthy eating habits, 183
  managing damaged skin, hair, nails, 180-181
  medications and nutraceuticals, 195
  mindful body scan, 191-192
  nail anatomy, 179
  progressive muscle relaxation, 191
  relaxation, 190-193
    breathing retraining, 192
    mindful body scan, 191-192
    mindfulness approaches, 192-193
    progressive muscle relaxation, 191
  self-compassion, 189-190
  skin anatomy, 177
  sleep duration and quality, 185-186
self-compassion, 20, 189-190
  founder of the movement, 116
  modeling, 21-23
  power of, 129
sensory domain, 38-39, 43
  overview, 86-87
  BFRB journey plan, 110
  intervention plan, 106
  logging BFRB activity, 107, 123, 144
  near senses, 104
    soothing interventions, 105
  oral/taste, 97-100
    example behaviors, 97
    increase positive sensations, 99
    intervention examples, 98-100
  smell, 100-102
    intervention examples, 102
  sound, 102-104
    intervention examples, 103
  touch, 92-96
    example behaviors, 93
    intervention examples, 93, 96
    tactile soothers, 96
  visual, 87-92
    common triggers for BFRBs, 88
    intervention examples, 88-92

shame, importance of addressing feelings of, 15
skin
  anatomy, 177
  health, 176-177
  managing damage to, 180-181
skin picking disorder (SPD)
  inclusion in DSM-5, 7
  prevalence in adults, 10
sleep duration and quality, 185-186
smell, 100-102
  intervention examples, 102
sound/auditory sensations, 102-104
stimulation levels, feeling over or under-stimulated, 141

taste and oral behaviors, 97-100
  example behaviors, 97
  increase positive sensations, 99
  intervention examples, 98-100
thought, categories of, 111
time of day, potential role in BFRB activity, 160
timing
  determining a good time to start your BFRB journey, 32-33
  role of in recovery, 31
touch, 92-96
  example behaviors, 93
  intervention examples, 93, 96
  tactile soothers, 96
Towhig, Michael, 117
"trance-like state," 36, 151
trichotillomania, *see also* hair pulling disorder (HPD), 7-8
triggering activities, examples of, 11

understanding your BFRB, 60-82
  ABC model of behavior change, 60, 64, 67-70
  action items
    High-Risk Situation Form
      completing, 63-64
      example, 62
    identifying
      cognitive barriers to recovery, 79
      relevant As, Bs, and Cs, 69
      the functions of your BFRB, 71-72
      learn about your behavior chains, 65-67
      list the positives of your BFRB and possible alternatives, 73
  "encouragers," 67
  finding positive aspects, 68, 70-73
  identifying risk situations, 62-64
  potential barriers to recovery, 74-78
    cognitive impediments, 77-78, 79
    emotional obstacles, 74-76
  relapse prevention, 80-81

Index

urges
    overview, 23
    defusing from action, 130
    describing like a journalist, 131–132
    learning to ignore, 133
    urge surfing, 133

values and valued living, 121
vision, 87–92
    common triggers for BFRBs, 88
    intervention examples, 88–92

willpower, 25

For EU product safety concerns, contact us at Calle de José Abascal, 56–1°,
28003 Madrid, Spain or eugpsr@cambridge.org.

www.ingramcontent.com/pod-product-compliance
Lightning Source LLC
LaVergne TN
LVHW080312260326
834688LV00038B/1077